*Please feel free to add your comments,*

*without any fear of reprisal...*

# biography

**SOCIAL COMMENTATOR OF WORLD RENOWN**

*Expert in Counter Intelligence and the gathering of information:*

Born near Haworth West Yorkshire.  Mother an English schoolteacher, Father unknown,
or major sponsor of the Guinness Corporation and member of Sinn Fein.
Occasionally attended a reputable Catholic Grammar school.
Bluffed his way into Art College (1975).  B A (Hons) Fine Art.
Signalman, Art therapist, and teacher of Sign-language.
In 2007 was caught in possession of a Browning semi-automatic revolver.

Winner of the Koestler award for literature.
Contender for the *Prix Goncourt.*
**Major novel (1996)**
**Short story writer and poet.  Political satirist.**
**Winner of the Welsh Open poetry competition.**
***Expounder of night terrors.***
***Professional arm-wrestler.***

BANNED DUE TO PUBLIC OUTRAGE

# NATURAL SURVEILLANCE

*Extracts from the world famous website and words of Landru:*

# INTRODUCTION

POEMS ARE LIKE CLOCKS FLOATING AROUND ON THE BREEZE AND WAITING TO BE OPENED. SOME ARE LIKE RHINOCEROS, SOME ARE LIKE THE SMELL OF MUDDY BOOTS.

*Please keep your insults confined to the page.*

*For Heather*

# DISCONTENTS

# Headmistress jailed for *predatory behaviour*

By Godfrey Winklebacker | Published: June 24, 2015 | Edit

If I had been lucky enough to have a teacher to give me first hand sex education at fourteen I would have counted myself extremely fortunate.  It certainly wouldn't have caused me to feel depressed or suicidal.

It's a disgrace that such a kind-hearted philanthropist should be sent to prison for eight years on the strength of statements made by grinning adolescent schoolboys who were only a few years younger than herself.

I suppose there is always the police bribe of thirty thousand or so to be taken into consideration?
The laughing gleaming ex-virgins must be old men by now.

Why would they want to make poor Mrs Lakey go through so much pain and suffering if it wasn't for skank and a good hand job from the Assistant Commissioner?

As we all know: sex is only right within a caring loving relationship, and between consenting adults...

# Home

Welcome to one of the most unusual and intriguing sites on the net:

The *Literature* section comprises a number of different *HIVES* each containing a selection of short stories, poems, and political satire.

There is also a section involving **Prophecy** and **Prediction**, **Spells** and **Invocations.**

You can also order your own personalised **ASBO.**

I have long considered writing to be a *form of art.*

The Artwork section contains pages from the *infamous* 'THUNDERBUCK RAM.'

**BELINDA'S HOT AIR gives participants of the site the opportunity to express their views on a very diverse range of subjects.   By clicking on the heading you can add your own comments, but you need to be signed in to *Facebook*.**

**FIRST CONTACT is a forum for new untested art forms and experimental writing.**

**In an age of increasing state control and monitoring your general comments and feedback are positively encouraged.**

**Our freedom of speech and liberal values have to be permanently fought for or else they are lost.**

***Live dangerously and to your heart be true.***

**Proxima Centauri Alpha**

***L0+4A***

# John Hinson: RIP

By Usuli Twelves | Published: June 24, 2015 | Edit

The acclaimed Yorkshire builder famed for his false contracts has died some two years after his legs were amputated. He might have been a corrupt businessman who duped the council out of thousands but he had a great appetite for food. I was pleased to hear that he left his entire fortune to his son in recompense for having to grow up in the same family as his sister. It is purely co-incidental that she married a Muslim and thought that all white men had tiny little dicks.

# Slashing legal aid

By Usuli Twelves | Published: June 24, 2015 | Edit

You might have guessed that the Tories would slash legal aid for the poor and needy. I'm in favour of *complete inequality.* Let's all just fight for the truth.

# Calais migrants hunting for space

By Godfrey Winklebacker | Published: June 23, 2015 | Edit

Thousands of men from across the Mediterranean with no home, job or means of support are desperately seeking a better life here in Britain. Why let them into Europe in the first place. Hasn't anybody heard of 'birth-control?'

If they do manage to crawl through the Channel tunnel it may seem as if they have swapped one dictatorship for another.

# <u>When to end life</u>

By Godfrey Winklebacker | Published: June 23, 2015 | Edit

A poor man lay suffering on his bed after the recent bombings in Yemen. His skin had melted and his lungs were burnt to hell. Yemen is a poor country. The Saudi's aren't. If I walked down the street and shot someone I would be arrested as a crazy psychopath. Put the poor man out of his misery. Put him to sleep someone.

What wonderful creatures we all are.

### HUGE RISE IN DEVIANCY AT WYMONDHAM CHICKEN PLUCKING FACTORY

By Adumla | Published: June 22, 2015 | Edit

Peabody has informed me that there's been a huge rise in the number of Officers straying off the straight and narrow and having to take early retirement from the force. The impact of shouldering so much power and responsibility has led many flat-foots down a long and sticky slope with no hope of a cure around the corner. I have complete faith and trust in his findings. It has long been my belief that they like nothing better than to have the rise taken out of them.

# Actual bodily harm

By <u>Rumplestiltskin</u> | Published: June 23, 2015 | <u>Edit</u>

We can now be charged with ACTUAL BODILY HARM for:

1.  throwing a biscuit (if it lands)

2.  cushioning someone from falling

3.  holding someone's hand

4.  shooting dead the *Home Secretary*

## The Anti Establishment austerity march

By <u>Rumplestiltskin</u> | Published: June 20, 2015 | <u>Edit</u>

There were about 150,000 protesters marching through the streets of London today in an effort to halt the raft of new austerity measures planned by the incoming administration. I imagine a very anxious Prime Minister cocking a smile down to the street below.

If you really want to get your face recognised by the Authorities then I urge you to join one of these demonstrations. The piglets gathered quietly in hushed tones behind their numerous barricades confident that their brethren sweating and crowding round the computer screen inside were photographing and filing away every last one of you for future reference.

# Storm Roof kills nine

By <u>Usuli Twelves</u> | Published: June 19, 2015 | <u>Edit</u>

Another Almighty American skeg goes on the rampage. In our country it's only the police who are allowed to carry guns and shoot people to high heaven.

# Pilgrimage to Mecca   by <u>Adumla</u> | Published: June 17, 2015 | <u>Edit</u>

A family of nine have courageously made it across the border into Syria. It may have been partly to avoid the children being taken into care by well meaning control freaks working for the British Authorities. Thank god the days of the British Raj and *backslapping Imperialist Red-necks* are finally on the wane. When will they get it through their thick heads: young Muslim men are not disillusioned because they want a better job: they are joining ISIS because they have rejected the ways of the West. These young men are fighting for an 'ideal,' not a new sports car and are prepared to sacrifice their life in freedom's cause to do it. To describe them as *lacking intelligence* or a good education is somewhat arrogant and patronising. Most Muslim men I have met have been extremely bright and shrewd. What they really don't like is POLICE HARASSMENT AND BULLYING. The surveillance culture we all have to endure day after day. In other words they would rather die than live in a country where oppression and snooping is a way of life. For the British Government to accuse ISIS of barbarity is a bit rich coming from a nation who shipped its propaganda and warfare all around the globe.

If there is a "flawed cause" then surely it must be the 'Peace Movement.'

## Police helicopter in search for dangerous fox

By Adumla | Published: June 17, 2015 | Edit

As I was sunbathing in my garden yesterday I observed another police investigation vessel speeding across the sky to see if I had my knob out.

No such luck fellas!

However, I did have some letters arranged in large print on the lawn:

'IF YOU CAN READ THIS YOU MUST BE  extremely thick'

# Zoo swamped by flood waters

By Adumla | Published: June 16, 2015 | Edit

A lot of very nice bears and wolves have died while trying to escape their captivity.  I can't think why they were trapped in their cages in the first place unless it was so that tourists could gape at them through their iron bars and throw pieces of bread.

Several of the man-apes were seen racing around with shot guns.

I hope no-one gets bitten…

# The dangers of sexting

By Sarin | Published: June 15, 2015 | Edit

I am a firm believer that it is unwise to send sexual messages while you are driving.  While you are masturbating is fine!

# Hillsborough

By Sarin | Published: June 15, 2015 | Edit

"It woz the football 'ooligans wot done it Yr Hon'r!"

# Little Jack Shit to join Slipknot

By Sarin | Published: June 4, 2015 | Edit

Yes, another member is soon to join the band.  Douglas Carswell is first in line but Martin Keown is knocking on the door.  Masks freely available!

Comments

# Nanny required: WYMONDHAM SPY CENTRE

By Godfrey Winklebacker | Published: June 10, 2015 | Edit

ESSENTIAL:

1  Ability to blindly follow the instructions of your ***Commanding Knob-head.***

2  Smart, cocky, ready to pounce.

3  Large Shrek-like hands and feet.

4  Qualified to kick in doors.

5  Know the alphabet.

6  A brown nose.

7  Able to look through key-holes.

8  Computer literate on all pornographic web-sites.

9  Slippery, two-faced and cunning.

10 Capacity to handle stolen goods.

11 Self loathing and a patronising intolerance.

PREFERRED:

1  A much higher than normal IQ for a pack animal.

2  Able to read, write and do sums.

3  Re-inforced steel toe caps.

4  Able to put on a disguise or funny voice.

5  Vengeful, mean and spiteful.

6  Able to partake in group *masochism*.

7  Ability to falsify records.

8  A flair for wit and persecuting others.

9  No lack of fear, prejudice or compromise.

10 A strong sexist attitude.

11 A helpful and gregarious nature.

12 Familiarity with all snooping methods.

13 Respect for jelly and other types of frogspawn.

14 The innate skill to spot a liar at twenty paces.

15 A tiny talking cock of the white variety.

\* *We employ a team of dedicated professionals who will stop at nothing to pry into your thoughts, prowl through your litter bin and expose your wickedness.*

# Mole caught with pants down again

By Godfrey Winklebacker | Published: June 5, 2015 | Edit

As predicted Peabody's small bungalow was raided at four in the morning just as he was standing up from his lavatory. All his documents, used underwear, and britches were placed into plastic containers and sealed up. He rang me at half past nine to say he had confessed to hiding a small *medium sized cigar* in his holdall on his way back from the clinic eighteen months ago. His phone had been tapped and all his relatives informed.

*A small myopic creature had emerged from the soil on the* **Wymondham Spy Centre** *lawn. It tried to wipe the mud away from its eyes with long and clumsy fingers. The creature proceeded to move slowly across the grass. Fat Belly shone a light in its eye and laughed. The mole just went around in circles so he stood on it.*

*A few mounds of earth were discovered near the main sewage pipe. "We really have you this time!" screamed Gumby.*

*"We're gonna make your life a fucking misery from now on."*

# Janet Street Porter has a point

By Sarin | Published: June 4, 2015 | Edit

I rarely agree with loud-mouth Janet Street Porter, but on this occasion I think she is right. What is going to happen when parents are arrested for smoking in front of their children, for being obese, or for answering back an Officer of the Law?

# Never apologise

By Sarin | Published: June 4, 2015 | Edit

Never apologise for actions made in the past no matter how much pressure is placed on you. The decisions you made in days gone by were based on how you were then. Do not fall into the 'guilt' trap! *Feeling guilty's* for Smeg-heads.

Comments

# Stansfield no ordinary crook

By Usuli Twelves | Published: June 3, 2015 | Edit

Listen here people.  There is more than just one side to a story.

It's simply not true that I am a **groping perverted sex-fiend**.

Ask Peabody.

# Bring back the Coliseum

By Sarin | Published: August 20, 2015 | Edit

Today's entertainment is really boring compared to the Roman games.

Bring back the bull fuking prostitutes and Christian sacrifices I say.

# Social media sites censored by Government

By Rumplestiltskin | Published: May 30, 2015 | Edit

**I've noticed in one or two cases recently that when anyone gets into trouble their page is taken down without any reason or explanation.**

**Why aren't we allowed to read what they have written?**

# Assisted suicide. Why fear the wrath of 'god?'

By Rumplestiltskin | Published: May 30, 2015 | Edit

Some British citizens who are also members of the Establishment are saying they would go along with 'assisted dying' as long as the decision was made by *twisted Creationists sitting in a Court of Law*.  To hell with the Courts.  I don't need anyone's permission to take my own life.  It should be a personal decision.  I wouldn't mind assisting Lord Falconer and one or two of his buddies though.  Some of them have been ill for a very long time.

**Mr High**

1 How long have you lived at Bure Valley Camp?

When you first moved in did Mrs Didwell or any other person say anything to you about me?

2 Why did you completely ignore me when I saw you in the Reception area for the first time and I simply said "Hello" to you?

May I remind you, you are on oath.

3 Have you ever been able to tell the truth?

4 Why do you think that me exercising in the garden on a bright sunny day is intimidation or harassment?  Did you ever report me for being in the garden. Was it you who called the cops?  WHAT A LOW THING TO DO.

5 Would you say that Mrs Didwell was a friend of yours?

6 You say you saw me walking down the corridor at night. Why should that be a concern to you? Is there anything wrong with walking down the corridor. You said that I looked towards your flat. That's wrong, isn't it?

7 I was waiting to go in the office one day when I overheard you. You were talking non-stop about me exercising in the garden for forty minutes. You don't like me?

7 At the Resident's meeting you rushed up and trotted after Mrs Didwell as soon as she left when she refused to stay in the meeting if I was there. You never came back?

8 You accused me of taking a motor-bike from the bike shed when the shed door was left open. Why did you accuse me and what evidence did you have?

9 You accused me of impersonating a member of Wherry Staff. I did not say I worked for them, ever. I simply told a new Resident that I ran a bingo and coffee morning and that I did work for the Residents sometimes such as cycle up to the shop on errands.

10 Have you ever colluded with Mrs Didwell about me? Why do you completely refuse to talk to me?

11 In your statement you accused me of damaging cars in the Parking bay. What evidence do you have? You do know that there is a law against 'Slander?'

12 What evidence do you have that these taps on the window are me (quite apart from your own prejudice)?

13 You said you saw me on my bike in town. I cycle all over town every day. You accused me of looking at you. Did I threaten you? Did I say anything? What have you got against me?

14 I have not threatened you or harassed you. It is all in your imagination. Why should I do a thing like that? You are probably suffering from what is known as 'a guilty conscience' for all the lies you have told about me in the past.

Are you seriously accusing me of 'looking at you?'

Talk about 'give a dog a bad name!'

# Human Zoo

By Godfrey Winklebacker | Published: May 11, 2015 | Edit

Yesterday *the Whispering woman* called to me across the car park. I thought I would let her know the truth about the Injunction so I wrote her a note.
She called the police and accused me of upsetting her. I'm now on my final warning!

## Comments

Mrs Didwell

**Sorry if we have ever disturbed you with any noise such as the smoke alarm going off. We didn't know how to turn it off at first. I did keep telling her to put the fan on.**

**When we realized you could hear us in the bedroom from your lounge we made strenuous efforts to keep the noise down. I know you sent in detailed accounts of our conversations there.**

**I apologise for us coming in late sometimes if that disturbed you, but that is a long time ago. We did sometimes cook a late-night supper, but I always made sure we kept the noise down and it was never excessive.**

**Just recently I did shut the door rather hastily because I was in a hurry. It was about 11.00 at night. I'm sorry if it caused you any distress. It certainly didn't go on for thirty five minutes as you claim.**

1 Do you remember the first time we met? You implied that 'Blondie at number 39' was nothing more than a prostitute because she got men to take her out for meals and she was known locally as "the Aylsham bike!"

Mrs Pigott is not a bit like that. She's a decent respectable woman from a good home and wouldn't hurt anyone.

2 Do you remember the second time we met?  <u>You asked me what I was doing at BVH.</u>  You said that people usually had to have something wrong with them to be in there.  You refused to speak to me again.  Why did you refuse to see the outside Mediator with us to sort out any issues you had in an orderly and adult manner?

3 Have you ever told anyone that you were "going to get rid of me?"  Did you ever say you would get rid of Robert Lilly?  Irene (Support Manager) said that you did and that you were "Nothing but a troublemaker!"

4 Have you ever heard anyone else say that they were 'going to get rid of me,' such as your friend Mrs Temple, or Mr. Yahman?

5 How often have you spoken to Mr Yahman?

6 Did you know that we can hear you and Bert shouting and swearing at each other all the time?  We have never reported you because we are not that petty.  And, we are not malicious.

7 Do you remember your husband discovering a live bullet in the laundry?  Do you have any idea where it may have come from?  Your son's a serving police officer isn't he?

8 Do you remember threatening us in the hall way in February 2013?  You said that you had a "good mind to bang both our heads together!"

9 In September 2015 you had a visit from one of our old neighbours Eileen (Number 32).  You used the opportunity to tell her that me and Mrs Pigott were having sex in the garden and that is why you had to put up your fence.  Is that true.  Do you know that is slander?

10 Do you know Mr High?  How well do you get on with him.   How often do you talk together?

11 I put it to you that we have never been bad neighbours and that you have serious issues with us which you won't discuss.  Are you prepared to finally say, here today, openly, what they are?

12 You are determined to label me as a nasty dangerous and disruptive person?  Why are you so concerned about me.  Have I ever threatened you or shown any aggression towards you?

I don't bear a grudge towards anyone no matter what they have done to me.  I'm not that sort of person.  I don't know what sort of person you think I am.

I'd like to question you in more detail about your complaints.

> Clause 14 paragraph 3 of your complaints to Mrs Harrison (29th April): You claim that I was banging on the wall at 04.20 am and that you heard me say "We'll get into trouble?"  You say you heard me laugh. This is a lie, isn't it?

> Clause 14 paragraph 4: You claim you heard a noise <u>which you think</u> came from number 39.  Can you be more specific? What makes you think it was me?

10th May 2015 (01.30-01.45): You claim I was making a noise and that you heard me say "I need bed now!"

Do you know that there is a punishment for *slander*?

**<u>I was not there and I have never stayed overnight since I left.</u>**

> Clause 15 (15th May) : You say I was seen carrying some laundry bags into the main building.  I have never done my laundry there since I left although I have carried some shopping in for someone and moved some rubbish.

> Clause 14 paragraph 4 (29th April) : You claim that you heard me banging the door repeatedly from 11.20-11.55 pm.  That's simply not true is it (although I probably went home about eleven that evening)?

> NB You say you are **'fearful of being at home.'**  This is deliberate myth-building.  I don't know who put that bruise on your arm, but it certainly wasn't me!  I'm not interested in you.  WE DID NOT STAND LOOKING INTO YOUR KITCHEN FOR FOUR HOURS.

I have never harassed you and you don't have anything to fear from me.   <u>Thank you for your 'honesty' in coming forward.</u>

## Marilyn

1 I'm sorry if the note caused you any distress.  I always thought we got along.  I simply wanted people in the home to know the truth and that I had not done the things some people have said I did.

2 You did once say that you would vote for me and no-one else when people were voting for the SHAP Representative.

3 By the way.  I did not have sex in the Reading room.  I had been doing some sit-ups on the floor when you glanced in as you passed and there was no-one else in there with me.  I heard you had been off your food for a week and had been vomiting *every five minutes*.

## I know something you don't know...

By Usuli Twelves | Published: May 9, 2015 | Edit

### FREAKS

By Adumla | Published: May 9, 2015 | Edit

Dear *Whispering-woman,*

Just a short note. I hope you don't mind me writing. You were always such a sweet and agreeable neighbour...

I have vacated the zoo due to:

1 BULLSHIT.

2 THE SHORT BALD CAMPER-VAN-DRIVER AND *HIS CRIPPLED MOTHER.*

3 SPYING.

4 THE LAUNDRY HOBBIT.

There are FAR better places to live than *Bure Valley Animal House.*

May I wish you and the 'Laughing gnome' a very happy life together.

# Pigs guilty of revenge

By Bird Dung | Published: August 21, 2015 | Edit

For a long time now the police have been getting very angry with people recording their pig ignorance.  It is in the public interest to see how these dwarf-brained morons go about their tyranny. As an act of revenge the police have decided to add yet another contraption to the ones they already have in every town centre and street corner.  It will be pinned on their life-jacket and will record every litter lout in the country.
Information will be stored away for the next five centuries.
How long before the Government brings in yet another new law to prevent us from recording **their activities?**

## Swine guilty of troughing

By Bird Dung | Published: August 21, 2015 | Edit

I would call them 'animals,' but that would be an insult to animals.

# Jeremy Kyle louts and dog breeders

By Usuli Twelves | Published: May 9, 2015 | Edit

Where does he find them all?  Apart from:

1  The local council estate

2  The dole queue

3 The prison gate

Love one another!  You must be joking.

## New police powers to bully workers

By Sarin | Published: May 21, 2015 | Edit

The police have been given new powers to confiscate the hard earned wages of migrant workers.  It was the Prime Minister who pushed this one through.  Another Tory boot in the groin.  No surprise there.

Comments

## Filipino insulin donor

By Godfrey Winklebacker | Published: May 19, 2015 | Edit

So 'justice' has prevailed. How come an innocent woman was sent to prison for six weeks if the jury system and police methods are so fool proof?

Comments

# Fisting Julian Clary

By Godfrey Winklebacker | Published: May 19, 2015 | Edit

All that fuss over a poxy little wedding cake. Why can't people just accept that the law is meaningless and that it can *never be fair*.  Statutes cannot cater for *every shade* of **opinion.** I refused to give a lift to a gay man the other day. It wasn't because he was a shirt lifting puffta either.  I will not have *anyone* wearing an Arsenal shirt in my car.

## Mole-toad calls in from Wymondham mud gathering lab

By Usuli Twelves | Published: May 29, 2015 | Edit

Peabody has been very quiet recently, so it was a delight to receive his recent documentation.  He handed me a brown paper bag marked 'TOP SECRET.'
"You've done remarkably well bruv.  This is far more than I could have expected, innit."
As a mark of respect he removed his Waffen SS Visor hat.
I'm a little annoyed he can never remember to wipe his boots on the mat.
Must be all that marching up and down to band music.

# ISIS get control of nuclear weapons

By Adumla | Published: July 3, 2015

When you have finished ranting on this tiny island in the corner of Western Europe Mr Prime Minister think about the number of Muslim countries there are in the world who will not forget your willingness to kill. Let's see you try to arrest all their 'radicals' in the future.

# Trump to win by a mile

By Godfrey Winklebacker | Published: August 14, 2015 | Edit

Donald Trump is set to take the country by storm. He might be 'divisive' but at least he knows how to use a comb and play cards.

# Brown advice

A bit like asking a Polar bear for the nearest seal sanctuary.

By Bird Dung | Published: August 16, 2015 | Edit

"Don't vote for Corbyn. He's unelectable."

## Vicious homicidal gunman not considered 'dangerous'

By Bird Dung | Published: August 17, 2015 | Edit

There are plenty of people rotting away in prison who never killed anyone and whose only crime was to be poor and lacking in contacts. In our country it's called 'Justice.'

# BLACK LIVES DON'T MATTER

By <u>Bird Dung</u> | Published: August 10, 2015

Not to US cops anyway.

A teacher stabbed by his pupil in a racially motivated incident said today:

**"Violence is NEVER right!"**

What.  Not even if you're one of the 'Good Guys?'

*A significant portion of his classmates approved of the attack:*

*(names and addresses supplied on request).*

# Fatherhood

By <u>Bird Dung</u> | Published: August 6, 2015

Brian had been drinking cider again when he began to reminisce.  His eyes became bloodshot each time he came back to the house and he started to make strange sniggering noises.  He told us about the fantastic times he'd had taking speed and nutting his head through plate glass doors.

"You're going to make a great father," I said. "Respect!"

Brian wanted to borrow some more money to make the brat just like himself.

When his mother refused to buy him another play-station for the days he had nothing else better to do he said she would never see her grandchild again and would not be invited up for Christmas.

## Better for girls

By Usuli Twelves | Published: August 13, 2015

Girls are out-performing boys in their A-levels and for the first time outnumbering men in British Universities. This is undoubtedly because women possess a much sharper intellect and a logical left-sided awareness. **Yvette Cooper** could become the first female leader of the Labour party after the recent backlash against Jeremy Corbyn. It seems that we must prevent Mr Corbyn from becoming leader at all costs because it would 'ruin the country.'
Having voted Conservative for most of my life I think I might actually vote for him now.
Cooper said: "Mr Corbyn is just another white middle-class *man*. He will stop us from changing the world."
Tony Teflon said: "To vote for Jeremy Corbyn would be like walking blindly over a cliff!"
"This is a dangerous moment in Labour's history."
Presenters on *Sky* compared Mr Corbyn's appearance to a character in Star Wars.

There's the left sided logic again!

# Man gets custody for dementia

By Rumplestiltskin | Published: August 5, 2015

**LAWS MUST BE OBEYED.** For 'the good of society' an eighty-eight year old man was sent to prison for two years in Norfolk, just for having an old shotgun in his car loaded with ammunition. You never see a British soldier being sent to prison just for carrying a gun, and he might actually hurt someone with it. The pensioner's housebound wife was left to fend for herself while he was photographed, finger-printed and dragged from pillar to post.

"Tell us what we need to know!"

"You don't have to understand a single f…ing word."

"All you have to do is put on the striped jersey."

**'The obsolete firearm was 124 years old and appeared very confused about the whole incident.'**

'BRITISH 'JUSTICE' AT IT'S BEST,' Your Worship.

*Well, what do you expect when you give a racket-of-chimps a truck-full of machine guns?*

## Scapegoat Trader in for 14

By Rumplestiltskin | Published: August 3, 2015

A slimy manipulative Bank Trader (Tom Hayes) gets fourteen years in prison. The whole essence of the Stock Market is to take risks, out-manoeuvre your opponents and lead them into bankruptcy. Ask any Politician worth his salt.

I can't understand what he's done wrong.

*"We're entitled to expect the same level of honesty from Bankers as we do from everyone else!"*

You're having a laugh aren't you?

## Hippy crack take that rap

By Rumplestiltskin | Published: August 2, 2015

Pedalling 'laughing gas' for recreational use will now carry a seven year custodial sentence.

Hey, surely that's a bit too lenient (you assholes!)?

I wonder if that's a "*blatant breach of International Law* too?"

# Showing on You-Tube tonight

By <u>Rumplestiltskin</u> | Published: August 1, 2015

- How to deal with persistent ass-wipes
  - Police gang call for further training on porn web-sites
  - Pinky and Perky learn how to dance
  - Mafia hoods widen search for cami-knickers
  - Hitchcock exposes nuisance Bitchcops

*Baldridge and Bitch sent packing

- Police harassment of pensioner with Alzheimer's

  Also: SAD

  **Beecraft**

  1. Two bee or not to be
  2. Beekeeper signs Register accompanied by choir of angels
  3. Beekeeper pursued by swarm of giant bees

  Born again Christian cu.t

## Acclaimed 'Book-keeper' finally brought to Justice

By <u>Rumplestiltskin</u> | Published: July 15, 2015 | <u>Edit</u>

The acclaimed 'Book-keeper' of Auschwitz Oskar Groening has finally been imprisoned after seventy years of normal living. Oskar is to be made a 'Scapegoat' for all the guards, Politicians, and Bakers who died a very long time ago. Groening commented that all human beings were *simply trying to look after themselves.* He refused to apologise for being human or for the murder of over 300,000 avaricious Jews. Once again 'Justice (whatever that is) has been served.' Proof, once again, if proof were needed that mankind is a moronic, spiteful intolerant cretin.

# Equality of men and women

By Adumla | Published: July 14, 2015 | Edit

I want to see **more inequality, not less**!  Why are men expected to do most of the gruelling outdoor labour work; because they are different.  No warm erotic little offices for him.

Why should everyone be paid the same when we all have different traits and abilities?

If women really want to have equality, then let's start with pensions.  Why do men have to work an average of five years more than women before they can retire?  A lot of men seem to die not long after that anyway.

# Tourists ordered home by Big Brother

By Usuli Twelves | Published: July 10, 2015 | Edit

Unarmed British tourists have been ordered home from Tunisia by this pouting arrogant Government.  The very same Government who spends millions of pounds on surveillance and will do anything it can to hand over yet more powers to the Authorities.  Why don't people simply tell Philip Hammond to mind his own damned business.

I think I know what the *Duke of Edinburgh* would say…

"We had no choice but to go back home."

Yes you did.  You could have accepted the risk and continued to sun-bathe unmolested by a contagion of Whitehall Goonies!

# The Cosby show

By Usuli Twelves | Published: July 8, 2015 | Edit

Bill Cosby cannot be tried for things he admitted to a long time ago.  The Fuzz-heads aren't allowed to investigate crimes which go back more than ten years in the United States.  I believe there is NO TIME LIMIT here in 'Great' Britain.  You can be thrown into prison just on the strength of an *accusation*, and it doesn't matter if it happened *a hundred years ago*.  ***But only if sex is involved.***  The moral of this story is to build more prisons, and staff them with semi literate Smegs as usual.  The Cabinet must be laughing their cocks off.

# Teenage girls

By <u>Adumla</u> | Published: July 1, 2015 | <u>Edit</u>

I heard today how two teenage girls inflicted more than a hundred wounds on an older not very attractive woman. The young women chose a number of household implements to torture their victim to death.

1 There's no room in this world for unattractive people.

2 You can always count on the herd to pick on anything weaker *or stronger* than themselves.

## Mother commits infanticide and then blames Jo Fritzl lookalike

By <u>Rumplestiltskin</u> | Published: July 18, 2015

A mother who murdered eight of her newly-born infants and then blamed it all on her father has finally come clean. She no longer claims the babies were a result of an incestuous relationship with her father conducted over a period of many vain-glorious years or that she was forced to have sex against her wishes on more occasions than she wished to remember. A Court in France has handed down a nine year jail sentence after finally hearing her *tell the truth.*
(That's about the same *time* Mrs Lakey received for 'educating' some of her pupils).
It works out at about a year and a bit for every suffocation.
JUSTICE HAS BEEN DONE!
Does anybody believe any of this shite?

# Dear Baldridge,

This is the e-mail address for which I was sent to Court. I never made any attempt to disguise who I was. I always told people it was me. It really amounts to bullying when the police can treat people so harshly for next-to-nothing. Could you please let me have a copy of the Register requirements. I don't have one and want to be clear about them. Has there been any recent amendments, alterations or further bull?

As far as the order is concerned I believe that I am:

1 Not to search for my ex partner or her family

2 To give you access to any computer I have so you can snoop through all my internet activity

Is there anything else?

As I have said to the police on numerous occasions: I am not the person you take me for. This is just your 'label.'

My original offence was phone contact only, six and a half years ago. It was not threatening or malicious. I was not charged with anything sexual or violent. I might guess you would be eager to talk to me after the recent Court-case, in which I was accused of not declaring all my on-line aliases. I was correct in thinking too, that you would leave it a few days before you *sneaked around to the back door.*
* I see you brought your daughter with you this time. Could you possibly ask her how much she charges?

By <u>Rumplestiltskin</u> | Published: July 15, 2015 | <u>Edit</u>

# Solicitors part of the problem

By Godfrey Winklebacker | Published: June 27, 2015 | Edit

Once again I'm quivering on the edge of my marble column. The real problem is not the slashing of legal aid, but the nepotism among workers in the legal industry who all belong to the same conventional little cliques. Most companies would rather share information with the Authorities than represent anyone who did not conform to *their* perception of what was right.

That's supposing you could get one to represent you in the first place.

## Beach shooting: many dead/population still out of control

By Godfrey Winklebacker | Published: June 27, 2015 | Edit

## Biggest little bitches on the planet

*Mr Cameron* and the *Duke of York* were attending the **Armed Forces day** when news broke about the terrible beach massacre in Tunisia. Mr Cameron gave me the impression that he would stop at nothing to silence the voice of young Muslims in Great Britain who want to fight for an Islamic nation. He was adamant that these aspirations were exceedingly bad and that these young people had been manipulated by evil fundamentalists hell bent on the destruction of the West.
I suppose that will mean more radicalization from the Home Office and ever more penetration by teams of surveillance cops.

## Christianity to blame for warped viewpoints

By Godfrey Winklebacker | Published: June 27, 2015 | Edit

When you start building your legal system upon a religion which has basically stood truth on its head you are seriously in trouble. Christian views have given people a twisted view of what life is all about.  It is not about 'saving' everyone on the planet from dying, loving every loathsome creature who ever existed or preventing violence. War is a natural state for mankind to be in.

# American prisoners on the run

By Godfrey Winklebacker | Published: June 27, 2015 | Edit

The American Justice system has been appeased: one of the prisoners on the run has been shot dead. About eight hundred police plebs are searching for the other escapee. You aren't allowed to get away at any cost and if you do try to escape you will have a further ten years added to your stretch.
These wonderful human beings are really something aren't they? On a similar point: same-sex marriages are to be allowed right across the United States. I would have thought a relaxing of the gun laws must be the sensible conclusion?  What *moralistic claptrap*!

# Bunderchook accused of having sex in garden

By Godfrey Winklebacker | Published: June 27, 2015 | Edit

It has been alleged that the Good Doctor has been having carnal relations in his back yard again. This is totally against group ethics. A neighbour heard him talking over the garden fence and immediately reported his behaviour to Special Branch.

# Violent crimes against women

By <u>Godfrey Winklebacker</u> | Published: June 26, 2015 | <u>Edit</u>

There's been a huge increase in the number of violent crimes against women or so the Ministry of Vital Statistics would have us believe. The number of violent crimes against men by women over the last few centuries can't yet be validated. I was always brought up never to hurt a woman, yet I would ask Alison Saunders this: 'do women *ever* lie?'

She called the figures: "the very tit of the ice-berg!"

Some of the cases of violence include:

* on-line text messages
  grooming your horse
  voyeurism
  nudity

* slapping the bum

* groping a breast (even if it's your own)

NB  I wonder if these stats include people like **Dave Lee Travis** who was eventually found guilty of one offence out of twenty (second time around).  The Crown Prosecution Service must have been having kittens he was going to get away with them all. If you subtract all the crimes committed by Jimmy Saville OBE (although never charged or prosecuted for anything under the British Justice system) there would be about ten left.

# Sperm bank

By <u>Usuli Twelves</u> | Published: July 7, 2015 | <u>Edit</u>

My friend Mark works at the sperm bank.  He told me that he flushed many of the specimens down the bog and replaced them with his own highly dubious bodily fluids.

I can only take my hat off to him!

<u>STILL NO BOUNDARIES FOR BUNDERCHOOK</u>

A big fat FUCK OFF TO PHILIP HAMMOND then.

# Tony Blair has throat cancer

By Usuli Twelves | Published: July 7, 2015 | Edit

I have worried for years that there is something wrong with Tony Teflon's vocal chords. He said today that 'London could be justly proud of its record.' I presume he was talking about its record on Justice and Human rights, not to mention its treatment of ethnic minorities.

# Stephen Bett

By Usuli Twelves | Published: July 7, 2015 | Edit

**Stephen Bett,** your son is a disgrace but he is nothing compared to the liars you represent on a daily basis.

## What leads British Muslims to commit such extreme acts of violence and aggression?

By Usuli Twelves | Published: July 7, 2015 | Edit

POLICE HARASSMENT AND AGGRESSION

POLICE BRUTALITY AND INTRUSION

STATE TYRANNY AND EXTREME INTOLERANCE

## Nasty screw battered to death

By Adumla | Published: July 3, 2015 | Edit

Justice is a funny thing you know. GOOD TRIUMPHS OVER EVIL ONCE AGAIN!

## Angry Hitchcock exposes nuisance Bitchcops

By Rumplestiltskin | Published: August 1, 2015

We had old Baldridge and his Mrs up again on Thursday wanting to know how many times a week we shagged and if we always used a condom. Waving his hands wildly in the air and attempting to block the camera he asked why we felt it necessary to record his lugubrious activities. He said he had a lot of vulnerable people to protect and that the British Public seeing him on **You-Tube** would compromise his extremely well paid form of harassment. I said I was recording him for my own *protection*. You never know when the Smegs are gonna get you down on the floor or make up porky pies. I asked him if I had committed any crime. He said that someone had seen my cock half a century ago.

He accused me of refusing to 'interact' with them both in a manner which was conducive with his own warped and twisted outlook. Baldridge barked down at me again.

His Mrs said that the Solicitor they had arranged for me had told me I could not film them. I said this was absolute garbage. I don't know her name, but I guess she must be on the pay-role too.

Once again I read from the original charge sheet: phone contact, non malicious or threatening. F~king Groundhog day!

I asked them to tell me what offence I had committed to be placed on this Register. They refused to comment and continued to heckle me in the hallway. You have a *SOPO* order!

"Let's stick to the facts," I said. "The truth is that I did not commit *any* offence to be placed on the Register, and you know it!"

I told them that they were not coming into our home laying down the law and that they could stick my label where the monkey stuck its nuts.

I tried to give them a list of my on-line identities but they walked away in a huff.

*Good riddance to bad rubbish!*

## Swarm of Tories invade House

By Rumplestiltskin | Published: July 30, 2015

A malodorous and gluttonous band of MP's has invaded the House of Commons and is heading for every failing council in the country. Be prepared for further invasions of privacy and for new laws to order you about.
This Home Secretary couldn't organise a piss up in a brewery let alone an Immigration Centre.

# Turkey grants American bombing of Islamic State

By Godfrey Winklebacker | Published: July 24, 2015

After refusing to get into line for years Turkey has finally granted the US the right to use its bases to attack Islamic State. Membership of the EEC and a 'Nobel' prize look like a formality. President Obama called it a "game changer." Glad you think it's a game Mr President. The anti-gun lobby are 'up in arms' again after another mass shooting. Would they seriously be complaining if it was a cinema full of Paedoes instead of a room filled with over-stuffed hamburgers?

## No more old drivers

By <u>Usuli Twelves</u> | Published: July 20, 2015

At last.  Someone has finally done something about the number of inept old age pensioners clogging up the roads.

# Government support the right to bear arms

By <u>Rumplestiltskin</u> | Published: July 19, 2015

It's okay to buy guns and shoot people if you are the incumbent Government.  That makes it alright.  Unless of course another Government intervenes.  It all depends who is the most powerful then.  I note with some scepticism the jubilant expression of the Prime Minister, who has now changed his mind about bombing the Muslims of Syria.  He's still very much against the carrying of fire-arms by decent law-abiding Citizens of course.

## Johnson pays for Water cannons

By <u>Rumplestiltskin</u> | Published: July 15, 2015 | <u>Edit</u>

In the House of Commons today the **Eton-albino** looked ready to stab May in the back with his pen.  Even a joke encouraging him to wash his hair with the contraptions seemed to go down like a lead-balloon.  Who knows though.  With a bit of luck the law might be altered again.  We could see striking picket-lines being sprayed in spunk as well.

# Fisher Cowe and Big Brother

By <u>Rumplestiltskin</u> | Published: July 19, 2015

## Dear Mr Cowe (Gavin),

I have finally got my property back but there are still a few things missing.  I have asked the police about them but they say they aren't being released. Please note:

1 A copy of a story written by one of my writing group about a serial killer (God knows why she wants to write about that sort of thing).

2 A CD which is years old.

3 My phone connector

Some files have been tampered with and some programme files are missing.

As I have said on numerous occasions.  I am not a Sex-offender and I did not commit any sexual offence to be placed on the Register.

Is there anyone in the country allied to the Establishment who is willing to take on these cunning and deceptive rascals?  I have asked them to give me a copy of the Register requirements and SOPO but they have refused.

When the Smeg-heads called to harass me again today they said you had told me I could not film them any more.  This is absolute kack.  You never said that, although I know they were in cahoots with the previous firm of Snitches.  My mum is getting very upset by their regular appearances.

Why can't you ever do anything?

Anybody would think you were on the same side.

*Comments?*

# Royal Family in pact with Hitler

By Rumplestiltskin | Published: July 19, 2015

For generations the Royal Family has given its tacit approval to fascist ideologies. How could anyone live in such opulence without believing in the survival of the fittest? The last time I saw Prince Philip eyeing up the local talent I suspected something was being swept under the carpet and it wasn't Prince Harry in fancy dress.

# Religious leader elected new Liberal party goat

By Rumplestiltskin | Published: July 19, 2015

How can an evangelical Christian be the leader of a party espousing liberal values and freedoms. Who could be more judgemental than an Evangelical Christian? A very poor choice of leader, yet probably more of a Liberal than Clegg.

# <u>Mary in a blue-grey gown</u>

I first arrived at Walsingham in the Spring of 2002 to look after Father Peter Allen who had been the Director of the holy shrine there.

For months whispers had been circulating round the village that he had taken to the drink.
People had seen him staggering home along the pavement.
Sometimes he'd been seen unable to walk properly as he made his way up the High street.
It was months later that he was finally diagnosed with **motor neurone disease.**
I heard people say that he would easily have been made Bishop if he had not become so poorly.
It is a frustrating illness, and one which was particularly hard to bear for someone so intelligent and refined.
The mind remains keen, but the body gives up hope.
I remember how particular he was about getting his nose patch in the right position before bedtime.
The mosquitoes were always getting in through the window during the night.
It was a close knit community of loyal and faithful followers.
I only realised after I had left that they were all members of a sect dedicated to the Virgin mother of God.
Priests and nuns paid us regular visits. Father Peter had friends who came to see him from all around the world.
Every week we held a very intimate and special Catholic mass in his bedroom. I was often being mistaken for the Deacon.
He conducted the mass in great pain but always embraced us at the end of the service. You could feel the love pouring from his arms.
I cycled down to the slipper chapel each day to lead the stages of the Rosary.
It was during the time of Soham; both girls had their pictures on separate sides of the altar.
My bedroom was on the first floor facing the garden and the wall which separated us from the upper road. Much of it was in ruin.
The friary had been built in the thirteenth century for pilgrims to stop off on their way to the shrine.
From the moment I entered my bedroom I could feel the presence of something not quite normal.
For days this feeling went on. I slept alone in the house except for Father Peter on the ground floor.
It did feel a bit spooky but nothing threatening.
I remembered being visited at home by the local Catholic priest when I was only a little boy. Father Murphy. That was in the days when Catholic priests were looked on with very high esteem. He used to have an occasional drink with my father

I was lying in my bed one morning at the friary. It was about half past seven. The light was already coming in from the window. I was on the cusp of sleep. Not quite awake. Still thinking. But I was conscious of everything in the room.
I felt the presence of a woman standing over near the wall. She was dressed in strange clothes. Not in any kind of dress I recognised. Her face was serene. It looked perfect. Her hair was in a style I had never seen before. She seemed neither young nor old. Her attire was neither ancient nor modern.
I was aware of her for some time before she suddenly started to move. She may have been there for a while.
It wasn't like any earthly movement. It was far swifter.

*As I lay in my bed she came over to me, bent over, and whispered something in my ear. I couldn't put together what she was saying; the words all seemed so fast;*
*like a speeded up tape recording. Like words from another world or another dimension.*
*I thought no more about it, but I recognised that I had been visited by someone. I opened my eyes.*
*I never felt her presence there again and never mentioned it to anyone.*

*It was not long after that I wrote my letter…*
*I never expected a reply.*
*About a month later a letter arrived for me at the Friary. I was over the moon when I saw it.*
*Father Peter was sitting at his computer in his large bedroom overlooking the drive. I placed it at his table in front of him.*
*For ages I paced back and forth. I kept returning to see him. There didn't seem to be any reaction at all.*

*Suddenly Father Peter began to cry. Great big tears rolled down his cheeks and he began to sob uncontrollably.*
*I wondered if I had done something bad.*
*It was from the Vatican, from Pope John Paul, who was extremely sick himself at the time:*

*''The Holy Father received your kind letter and has directed me to reply in his name.'*
*'His holiness appreciates the sentiments which prompted you to write and he invokes God's abundant blessings upon you and Father Peter, Society of Marius.'*
*Johannes Paulus*
*July 2ⁿᵈ 2002*

*After a while Father Peter stopped crying…"Thank you Andy!" he said.*

**In memory of Father Peter Allen 1937-2005 RIP**

I never told the Pope about the 'Visitation.'

# Floaters

Have you ever noticed the floaters in the top of the basin sometimes.

Someone ought to do something about them.

## Obama says climate change on the way

President Obama claimed today that climate change could mean millions of people would be displaced from  small islands in the Pacific.  Of course, they will all need to be rehoused somewhere… unless someone can come up with a radio-active teapot.

# Widening Underground

Once again they mentioned the items found under the floorboards:  a rosary from the nuns at Walsingham, my sacrificial dagger, a bottle of chloroform,  a roll of bicycle duck-tape with which to gag her mouth, a length of washing line to hang my victims on, and a pair of her knickers (had I been wearing them?).  I was warned that many more charges would soon to be added to the list.

# BROOKE OF SHOES

Mended,

As we cooled our heels,

On tip-toe to the nearby step,

The scent of rose and the patch of Elm,

The spill of gum,

The bake of leather...

Tours of those bygone lanes,

The strident arch at sixes and sevens,

Broad laces long and short,

Crammed in brown paper,

Pointed in black

Rimmed like swords,

And rounded in bronze...

We fetched our bags,

Swinging alongside and outpouring.

The drudge of our clogs,

Patterned with wanders,

And the stretching of corks into the chapel,

The cobbled stone of our life-blood,

Leaking our soul,

Over the tongue of our chambers.

But never in singles the pump of our braces,

Covered and dragged along acres,

The rub-rubber-wood,

Our slip-upons,

White in the foment...

Worn-out we pull-in,

Close to our woollens,

To gaze in the grace of the Drifters.

## The bigger picture

'Let's get this clear! Once and for all.' I snapped.

'One phone call.'

'One text message' (disputed)...

My key worker ploughed on with his pen,

That mighty brain of his doing over-time.

'We have to look at the bigger picture!' he smirked.

'You are dangerous,

a menace to society, and a MAPA level 3.'


# Astonished by the softness I feel


Our hands embraced, all through the service...

This is wrong she whispered,

You are very bad.

As we ran through the rain our fingers touched,

This is wicked Andrew,

And you mustn't.

Her voice rang out like a church-bell in the tender heart of the city,

On the cold grey seat where we huddled.

With eyes as big as saucers she spoke of childhood tresses,

Her dainty shoes, like two white mice,

Gleaming, and savouring every word.

 Are you a gunrunner,

Do you have a deal to make,

Why do you keep running off like that,

Why do you have to go so suddenly,

Andrew?

Bitterness like cast-iron,

Unforgiving, brittle, and light,

Unsparing.

My hand sank like a leaf to her skirt.

No one knew poetry like she did.

# Split the clouds with leather

He split the clouds with leather,

My dad did on the road,

In the sunshine,

In the evening.

He booted it so high.

'It came down wet!' He cried.

## Why train-drivers are better for headaches than doctors

I've been thinking for a while,

That train-drivers are far better than doctors at curing headaches.

They get to the pain instantly.

Never ask any embarrassing questions.

They don't mess around with unnecessary pills,

You can't have anyway...

And their remedy is nearly always permanent.

There are no time-consuming phone calls to make,

Although an appointment time is crucial.

You may have to sit around for a few minutes,

But every cloud has its silver lining.

# I fear that Ishmael's head may still be shrinking

I fear that Ishmael's head may still be shrinking,

And it wasn't too big to begin with.

I fear that the staff,

Are stealing in at night;

Removing the brilliant substance of his thoughts.


I fear that Ishmael's head may still be shrinking,

He's tall and thin,

And soon he'll be all gone.

But that leaves his *indeterminate sentence,*

A long one we can all rest assured.

# Might turn out like Andrew

I was at my granny's funeral,

A sad affair really,

But we'd seen it coming a mile off.


We were standing out of the draught,

Along the side of the house,

When I heard it...

"...might turn out like Andrew!"


What was that?

# The harrowing manes of Stephen Plex

In Keighley,

The town where I was spawned,

There lived a youth I never met,

Yet,

His name filled me with complete and utter terror.


Along the dismal streets we trolled,

In the evenings:

Train spotting,

Bird watching,

Or just examining the facts of life…


My Uncle shouted: "Plex!"

"Plex!"

"Plex!"

I soon learnt to holler the alarm.

 We shot like streaks of piss in every direction.


V *"Her ass was this wide!"* v

Hello, my name is Heinrick.

I am the sixth cousin twice removed of the Dutch master known as Rembrandt,

and I have just murdered my daughter.

Her body is lying back there in the chapel. We had thought about ending her life in the barn, but we didn't like the thought of the horses having to tread in all the damp.

It was my wife, this rather fine example of Flemish beauty standing by my side who first suggested the idea.

We had warned my daughter about her table manners on many occasions, but she didn't seem to take the hint.

I could not in fact repeat some of her comments.

We are *extremely* sad to have been forced into this, but the *good book* states quite categorically that all offspring should honour their fader and mudder...

My poor wife has been beside herself with grief.

We lost two of our chickens last week to a fox which had been hovering outside the farm for days.

Peter will just have to take some time off from clearing the yard of *guano* to shift the body.

He's a bit of a layabout, but I might think about putting an extra gilder or two in his pocket.

Do you think that's enough?

Should there be more bodies...

My weak and skeletal arms droop by my side.

I have a surprise planned for my dearly-beloved after her supper.

I feel my face itching to laugh.

There but for the grace of God!

You think me chicken-hearted?

Look, I'll put it to you this way.

My brother was a vampire, my sister was a vampire, and we are all extremely famished.

Is that laughter I see creeping like the last stretch of an arm all over you?

She was like that too, our daughter.

Maybe I should do this for a living...?

**Conclusion**

**Luxury yacht**   By Adumla | Published: May 1, 2015 | Edit

I borrowed the keys for a luxury yacht while I was in Wroxham yesterday.   Brian the 'Badger' and Evelyn Muppet loitered outside.   I could see Brian stomping around impatiently drawing on his electric cigarette through the back door while Evelyn tended to her grinning and increasingly spoilt brat.   The brat smiled from her pram.   Another productive member of society who would one day take on the reins of power and a place in the dole queue.   I'm bitter.   I know it.   There's a long waiting list for the 'JEREMY KYLE SHOW.'

I'll put them forward.

## HAPPY AS A PIG IN IT…!

## Battle of the sperm
By Adumla | Published: May 1, 2015 | Edit It's *that* simple!

## Police harassment and bullying on You-tube

By Sarin | Published: May 2, 2015 | Edit

Pinky and Perky learn how to dance

Mafia hoods widen search for cami-knickers
How to deal with persistent ass-wipes
Police gang call in for further training on porn websites
SAD
Police Harassment of Pensioner with Alzheimer's
Police Harassment of alleged Sex-offender
**Plebgate…**
By Usuli Twelves | Published: November 4, 2013 | Edit

Old Vaz had their number: sounded like complete *fantasists!*   Where have I heard that phrase before…?
They're pretty good at walking all over little people, but when it comes to select committees…
Can't help feeling Mitchell used the wrong adjective to describe them though…!
**Cool son**
By Usuli Twelves | Published: November 1, 2013 | Edit
So they were at it night and day.   I think this has a lot to do with career envy.
Let he who is without guilt cast the first stone!
**Pigs!**
By Godfrey Winklebacker | Published: October 29, 2013 | Edit
By pigs, I suppose you mean a farmyard animal…yes, it's ok for them to hack into messages or carry firearms on the Underground, but if you or I did it…
I see Brookes is up for it soon.
I do hope Dave doesn't disgrace himself by sobbing away in the gallery.

# Stalker gets his cumuppance

By <u>Sarin</u> | Published: May 6, 2015 | <u>Edit</u>

When I read about Ken Ward being sent to prison for five years *just for* masturbating outside his neighbour's home I thought there must be more to this case than the Authorities would have us believe. As far as I'm aware **he didn't touch or threaten anyone,** so why such a long sentence?

Why don't we ever hear the other side of the story, or is that against the law too?

Newspapers print the most one-sided rubbish. I suppose they think flashing your cock is an outrage against *decent* society.

Why are Judges so ignorant? Is it simply because they couldn't care less? Whenever my neighbour decides to masturbate on our front lawn I always get the garden hose on her.

I was astonished by the harshness of his treatment, until I read that his victim, *Miss Rugmunchling*, was an ex police woman.

I'm convinced that the flat-foots view anyone who behaves like this as a monster and that if the death penalty was still available they would always call for it.

* In my opinion all he needed was a *mop and bucket. Help not hinderance!*

### 'Independence Day'

By <u>Godfrey Winklebacker</u> | Published: May 7, 2015 | <u>Edit</u>

What a great machine. Did you see the way it cleansed the planet of all those noisy and annoying man-apes.

### Temple has camera

By <u>Godfrey Winklebacker</u> | Published: May 7, 2015 | <u>Edit</u>

One of the Bure Valley snoops has been photographing us in the car again. Someone told her I had no tax or insurance. Another sealed envelope to the Plebs then.

## Polanski

By <u>Sarin</u> | Published: November 5, 2013 | <u>Edit</u>

Had a chat with Roman today. He's really pisse. off with the Fuzz.

A plane load of Detectives flown out to Geneva.

For what? I bet she enjoyed every minute of it anyway.

**If it was up to me I would have them all gassed and kicked right back to where they came from.**

# BRITAIN'S GOT NO TALENT

By Usuli Twelves | Published: May 27, 2015 | Edit

There must be thousands of people around the British Isles who have more talent than this crowd:

- **Greasy dandruff comb man**

- **Dancing dwarfs**

- **Amateur magician man**

- **Yet another dancing group**

- **Attention seeking camp act**

- **Balloon bursting terrier dog**

- **Ant and boring little Geordie pair**

- **Crazy knicker flashing teacher**

- **Rubber skeleto man**

- **Angry snarling Simon**

- **Scary sword wielding infant**

- **Bald bland impressionist**

- **Economic migrants**

- **A three-legged collie and someone dressed as a Copper-gram**

## Death of a madman

By Usuli Twelves | Published: May 24, 2015 | Edit

**Poor John Nash.**

**Flew through a window with his cash,**

**and his wife,**

**covered in glass.**

# Is God a ventriloquist?

By <u>Usuli Twelves</u> | Published: May 24, 2015 | <u>Edit</u>

A lot of the usual suspects were absent from the Jubilee Family church this morning. Bank holiday. The kids were sent to play in the pen. Marshal stood up in front and preached from Corinthians. He encouraged the congregation to use their gift-of-tongues. Several recruits responded. Then I heard *Professor Scrivens*. It definitely wasn't his voice. He was standing in the aisleway just a little over to my left. It sounded Arabic and very spooky. I'm sure he leads a double-life.

Comments

## WORKING FOR PUBLIC PROTECTION

By <u>Godfrey Winklebacker</u> | Published: May 24, 2015 | <u>Edit</u>

I've been Commander of the PPU for years now and by the time I'd reached the rank of Inspector my nose had been permanently dyed the colour of month old mouse droppings. Please do not feel sorry for me. It was all in the line of duty.

I like to think I run a good team and that we all sing from the same hymn sheet, but Fat-belly is really getting on my tits. Just because he works in a pig sty he doesn't have to smell like one.

I caught him rubbing up against Sharon at our latest get together and Gordon informed me that he has been taking his work home…

I called him into my office. He came in my office.

I pulled my knickers up so fast I almost sliced through an artery.

Case Managers love a good kick in the balls now and again.

"Fat belly," I salivated. "It's nothing personal, but you need to wear a longer pull-over. I can see your big hairy gut and it's making me want to gag."

"**Do not take your work out of the building** on any account. I don't care if Judge Timothy wants to share your indecent images of *little boy scouts.*"

Fat belly gleamed.

I made a note of his reaction on my Facebook page.

"I want those dirty gits brought to book at all costs.

Take these instructions and pin them to the notice-board:"

**GUMBY** – lavatories, subways, and park benches.

**GINGER-MINGER** – Play grounds, zebra crossings, and school parking.

**FAT BELLY** – libraries, aquariums, and retards.

* Always go in two's and don't talk to any car park attendants.

# Russel Brand

By <u>Adumla</u> | Published: May 23, 2015 | <u>Edit</u>

**A thug with a syringe and half a telephone directory.**

# Good and bad Omens

1 Her son was a supporter of the 'Gunners.' Need I say more?

2 When we went to buy a car I thought I was buying a gold coloured Mitsubishi Warrior, which turned out to be silver because I'd had my sun-glasses on. It also had the letter 13 in the number plate.

3 We were invaded by flies all summer from the nearby fields. They were all over the house. I was vacuuming them up in thousands.

4 Her son attacked me with a toy sword when I came out of the bedroom late one night.

5 We burnt my Thoth tarot card deck in the garden.

6 Her mother said I was "not presentable"- I wasn't a Barrister or a Surgeon like her brothers, or a Chartered Accountant like her ex-husband, the very same one she had arrested because he refused to have sex with her ("there's no way I'm putting 'this' in there again..."). Mater told me that she gave Crow "dollops of money whenever she asked for it."

7 I gave her daughter a little tin doll for her birthday and she burst into tears. A bright funny little girl and I miss her.

8 Crowmarsh suddenly turned up at my place of work early one morning with a pink letter addressed to me. I was concerned that her stalking-behaviour might have returned. We had only known each other two days.

9 She made me late getting back to work for the first time ever because she refused to let me out of the house until I'd had sex with her. It was during one of her periods.

10 I caught her dancing to her Michael Jackson records in the middle of the night in the kitchen. It was about the same time as his trial.

11 She asked me to verify if her breasts were still producing milk even though her daughter had been born six years earlier.

12 She told me she had once stalked her ex boyfriend to Spain only to find his new partner at the door. She told me that she was very flat chested and that there was *nothing there*. She had met him while treating him as a patient when she worked as a nurse in London.

13 She once drove us through the traffic lights at red, screeched to a halt and shouted "bread!"

14 I found an extremely large frayed patch in the crutch of her black knickers.

15 I discovered some messages on my phone:

   ✓ *I love you dearly*

   ✓ *I think you have a beautiful nose*

   ✓ *Shall we get married?*

16 The 'thing' disappeared from under the stairs. She asked me if I thought her former mother-in-law had taken it...

17 She talked a lot about Aspergers.

18 She turned up out of the blue one morning with two sets of willy-pills. She ran a clinic on sexual health in the evenings.

19 I found she was on the pill, and an empty jar of Prozac.

20 Sometimes she found me asleep on the bathroom floor, or in the other room just like her ex-husband.

21 Crowmarsh had a series of lodgers. It was their friends in and out of the house I was more worried about.

22 She came to our work barbecue and sat down on the grass. The inside of her thighs were covered in terrible bruising. She said she had got them riding her old bicycle, so I bought her a *brand new one to go out on at the weekends.*

23 The shoes which I left at the side of the bed were always still there when I came back...

24 She fell into a coma one night and I couldn't rouse her, so I spread little tears all over her eyelids.

25 She was always wanting her back scratched, but she hardly ever offered to scratch mine.

26. I went along to church with her and the kids and tried to fit in with her wishes. Someone remarked that we weren't married so we shouldn't be living together. Crowmarsh suddenly started saying she wouldn't go to church if I was going....

27. The little black cat came in and licked between our feet each night. He was my favourite cat for ages. He meowed like mad the night I went in and found her collapsed on the floor with a broken wine glass.

28. Crowmarsh began chain-smoking in the garden. It was the first time I noticed a hard look in her eyes.

29. She said she wasn't happy at work so I suggested she did a course in *Osteopathy*. I even helped her to fill in the application forms.

30. Eventually I gave up trying to take her son back to his bedroom so he stayed with us, and then when the daughter saw this she had to stay as well, with her favourite cuddly toy 'Catty' which actually looked more like a mouse. I believe it's called 'pigging...'

31. She told her college chum (Anna) that Chowdry was 'very sexual.' I questioned Chowdry myself about this but he was rather coy. 'Just friends' he said. 'I stopped over a few times.' He seemed to encourage her behaviour. He said that in most relationships one person always liked the other more... Crowmarsh rushed around with a flushed face changing the bed sheets in her son's room....but she was back on the net the next night all on her own.

32. When I took Crowmarsh out to the local pub I was gob-smacked at how anyone could keep missing the dartboard like that. It had to be a different pub to the one where she was so well known. That was up the road into the next village.

I drove off and left her in the pub once. She knew I was going to do it. I just couldn't seem to talk to her. I still picked her up again as she walked up the road by herself. I felt *very* sad.

33. Her 'housekeeper' said that she and her husband had been intervening regularly during the last four years of her marriage to keep them both together.

34. I asked Rachel if she would like to take part in a three-some, and after a moment's hesitation she said 'yes.'

35. I was shut in the other room while she talked on the phone long distance. All I could hear was "yes friends...you're the best friend I have ever had! I know you are having trouble with your wife." It all sounded very intense.

36. Her son told me that the reason his dad left was because his mother shouted a lot.

37. Crow visited a lot of poor families in her job and took great delight in reporting them if she suspected any abuse...it didn't seem to matter what happened to them as a result.

38. Her skin felt like rubber. I didn't know if I liked it. She said it was her Maltese parentage.

39. I asked Crowmarsh what she meant when she said that she had 'only used men for sex when she came back from Saudi and was living in London.'

She said she had 'never said it,'and that 'there wasn't that many!'

40. She bragged to Chowdry about being a 'Scorpio' and about her activities at the church in Islington.

41. Crowmarsh started following me round at the weekends and wouldn't let me out of her sight, just in case I wasted myself doing something I shouldn't be doing....

42. I was once caught with a stink bomb under my desk.

43. We were on a trip to Windermere aged about twelve when one of my classmates spotted a bookstall with a mucky book rack. None of us had ever seen one before. Quite tame by today's standards. Since I was the only one brave enough to go and buy one they all clubbed together to give me the money. The precious cargo was smuggled on board the Lakeside ferry in my satchel and taken down to the gent's lavatory. I handed it over to my classmates who tore the book savagely to pieces. Never heard anything like it. A pack of ravenous wolves....the noise in there as they fought for a piece of the action.

On the way back to school in the minibus the book once again re-emerged from a bag but had been whittled down to just a few torn scraps.

Mr Jarvis who was driving saw something was going on in his mirror and asked for whatever it was to be passed to him.

"Who's is this filth?" he demanded (I think my name was muttered by someone).

"Yours!" I replied.

Forty lines....

# comments

# Ant and Dec bushtucker trial

By Surloin Steak | Published: November 20, 2015 | Edit

Rats too clean!  Need more piss and mud.

## Bartok Duka, Albanian pig-farmer

'Tell me!' you said,
on entering the door.
"How many people have you raped?"

Your round head,
and tired eyes,
the lines down both your poor cheeks,
my young friend.

I helped to write your letters,
I taught you to play chess and checkers,
And now you have won a game,
you said (grinning):

"I shall be playing in front of the Queen very soon!"

*HMP Bullingdon*

# ***Wangling of Judges***

By Surloin Steak | Published: November 20, 2015 | Edit

Why must particular Judges be assigned to their 'speciality' cases?  What's fair about that?

# Too many questions Mr Chawla

How did we manage,
yes, we are locked-up,
do I have a sister,
will we be allowed home for Christmas,
what time is it,
do we have a 'panic' button,
is my name Irish?
Mr Chawla.

Maybe these joggers do have elasticated bottoms,
Have I ever been skiing in the Himalayas,
Do I remember Britt Ekland?
Mr Chawla.

Did my grandfather fight at Dunkirk,
What are we having tomorrow,
Does the Queen pay for the poppies,
And yes,
I do remember the little man in Benny Hill.
Mr Chawla.


# The Newton Enquiry

I strode to the witness box,
in my Air-Jordans,
pulled by their shifty eyes.

Judge Corrie shrewdly inspected my notes...

"When you wrote that,
the pigs drove past you,
in two panda cars...
did you mean:
-the slang for policeman
-a farmyard animal
-or something else?"

"A farmyard animal!" I replied.

On-the-run.

# Sepia toning

Precocious age burlesqued in brown,

I puzzle through the shoals,

For an old man taking snaps,

In singles or in crowds.


Champagne of each frozen trait,

Their silver flows of silk,

in the magic tray are stretched,

beneath each lending wave.


Evergreen towards the tide,

Sun drenched skins of wine,

Each pitchy leaf of gold composed,

In twigs of felted grain.


My finger on the trigger still,

Press gently once, then sigh,

I wonder who behind the glass,

Is missing presumed dead…


**September 1966**

*NEVER LET THE DEAD MAN CRY*

19 July 2013

Last week Mrs Pigott was abused by the Scowler from next door, who called her "a dirty old slut," when she was getting her laundry.

She also said, "you shouldn't be doing those sorts of things at your age!"

Christine was extremely upset by her remarks and came to me crying. She did not react at the time due to her good nature.

I would like an Independent assessment of the noise. It has already been established that we were not making any undue noise after Mrs Pigott was accused of slamming her door and talking late at night, earlier this year.

I do not live at Bure Valley.

I have never had any complaints about noise, but then, I am not surrounded by neighbours who have any grudge against me...

When I have been at MS Pigott's home we have always tried to be considerate, although the walls are very thin (which is not our fault). We should be able to watch television in the lounge if the volume is at a reasonable level.

We do not have any trouble with normal friendly people. We have done nothing against the neighbours on either side, yet they have been instrumental in making Mrs Pigott's life a misery. I am at a loss to understand why they do not speak to us, because we have not done anything wrong to them.

We have had one or two barbecues recently and have been sunbathing in the garden. We were not noisy and our behaviour was *normal* at all times.

There is only one occasion which I can think of in the last few weeks where the neighbours may have had cause for complaint; this was when a smoke alarm went off. We were frying some mushrooms and the window was open, yet the alarm still went off. A smoke alarm is a safety feature which is not a reasonable cause for complaint. Her next door neighbour said she would be making a complaint immediately after this, and not before.

We did on this occasion open the door to help get rid of the smoke. We are sorry if this caused any annoyance to the neighbours, but if the kitchen was fitted with a modern air filter, then this situation with the smoke alarm would never occur.

We have made an effort to keep out of the way of her neighbours. If the neighbours didn't bear her such a grudge it would have been possible to talk to them like normal sensible adults instead of bad tempered ignorant twats.

Yours Sincerely,

**Gudrun Bunderchook**

Christine Keeler

PS My bike was interfered with. I hope it has nothing to do with son of Fat-ass.

# Watson women

By Surloin Steak | Published: November 15, 2015 | Edit

**I told my aunt that my mum kept charging into my bedroom in the middle of the night:**

"It's her home, she can do what she likes!" she sneered.  Another 'teacher,' another *bossy-britches*.

"I don't know what he's doing here.  We can't talk to Margaret when *he's* there," she gleamed.

"Why did you steal my mobile phone?"

"How dare he question me in my own home?"

# Simpson

As I have probably already explained: I did try to get a Solicitor as you suggested.
I even wrote to a few.
They either didn't bother to reply, or suggested I should find someone else.
I cannot get legal aid to deal with my problems.
This is the situation many people targeted by the police find themselves in.
If you remember, I was placed on the Sex Offender's Register, even though I had not committed a crime (my original offense was to contact my ex partner on the phone over nine years ago).
What is your Government doing to stop the police placing people on the Register for anything they can, such as a phone call, or a text message?
It may be funny to joke about in the House canteen but the case of Raoul Moat didn't make people laugh for long.
I was harassed again by the police again today, who kept banging on my door for ages and wouldn't go away.  I am in my fifty-ninth year and due to go into hospital soon.
They said that if I didn't let them in to search the place they would get a search warrant and break down the door.
They just turn up out of the blue every few days.
The neighbours are all talking about me because this happens so often.
In light of the recent cases (including that of the Deputy Speaker) what is your Government doing to prevent police harassment and bullying besides sweet fa?
I would be grateful if you would pass on my letter to the Home Secretary if that is not against 'Party protocol.'
**Not that she would do a darn thing!**
If something serious happens as a result of their on-going harassment then it will only be the fault of the Government. I am sure they are interfering in my e-mails, blocking some of them from being sent, and obtrusively examining my post.   What on earth is going on in this Country?
Incidentally, the creators of the Internet wanted it to be about 'freedom.'
You Tories certainly know how to brown-nose, don't you!

Yours Sincerely,

Mr Y.D. Ibother

## Dear Mr Simpson,

I am still getting harassed by the police nearly five and a half years after I phoned my ex partner and pleaded guilty to breaking a restraining order. I finished with her because I didn't want her.

They keep coming to my door and trying to bully me in front of my neighbours. I am not allowed to live a normal life and it is making me ill. As you say: the police are left to deal with Sex-Offenders and can do what the hell they like with them.

Please don't suggest writing to the Head of the Norfolk Constabulary again because we all know they piss in the same bucket, or of consulting with a Solicitor, when I already told you I can't get one. Not that they are any good at standing up to the Authorities any way.

Why is poor old Rolf Harris being tortured for a minor discretion which was over and done with decades ago?

You MP's are bloody useless.

No wonder people are turning to UKIP!

# Dear Mr Pratt,

I am writing to you again about the disruptive and intimidating nature of the police harassment I have been receiving for years. Once again they turned up at my home demanding to be let in (or they would get a warrant) so that they could go through my home, looking at all my personal items, checking all my bags, slavering in my wardrobe, scrutinizing all my private thoughts, snooping through my laptop, demanding I tell them who my girlfriend was, asking me all about my private life, looking at all my private letters and photographs. They sit down as if they own the place with a smug smile on their face while the neighbours gossip outside the window. I keep telling them to leave me alone but they keep turning up out of the blue, making me poorly and extremely annoyed for days.

Once again I told them today that my original offence was contacting my ex partner on the phone, on one day, nearly five years ago, and that it was neither malicious nor threatening.

Last month I applied for new passport. I wasn't intending to go anywhere, but wanted to use it for *identification.* They turned up to arrest me because I had not taken it in to be registered at North Walsham Wank station.

Last year they arrested me after I had forgotten to log off at the Central library and threatened me with five years in prison (which I could do without!). Then they had to let me go.
My partner was at her wits end today worrying they were going to take me away if there were any signs that I had tried to look for my ex partner (who left with all my property) on my computer (we broke up because I did not want her). Thankfully I aren't that stupid.

**I am a Writer and Artist. They took copies of all my work with them and 'cloned' my computer. They downloaded all my work onto one of their memory sticks. What has the Members of Parliament in this Democracy been doing to allow them such unhindered access to our private thoughts and space?**

This cannot go on. Who can help if not a Member of Parliament.

They turned up at the end of my sentence for the phone call business and told the Magistrates I was a dangerous Sex-Offender who would try and rape my ex partner or a member of the public. When I stood up for myself and said it was "Absolute rubbish!" I was accused of being 'aggressive.'

**COMMENTS?**

# Return of the Fabulous Flash

We had completed all the necessary paperwork.

Letters had been posted. Members of the public scrutinized.

Church wardens notified. Library officials put in the picture.

The worse mug-shot we could find was handed round to the press.

In the conference room the team stared up at the screen.

Grant!

You sure are an ugly twat.

Grimshaw guffawed. Wilkinson jumped from his chair.

"When will he be out sir?"

"Far too soon!" I replied.

I was pretty sure that all this rehabilitation bullshit wasn't going to make a scrap of difference.

My gut instinct: the *evil gene*.

We placed ten of our best detectives in the Forum.

They were spaced all along the chairs and tables adjacent to the computers.

The hotline phone rang at half past eight.

It was Reginald Glee again.

That damned phone never stopped ringing sometimes.

Webster followed him down from the hostel. Vicky watched him lock up his bike and walk up the steps.

The Copters were all buzzing overhead. I love the sound of their rotating blades.

Every route out of the city was blocked.

"Danger money!" I snarled. "Under resourced and over stretched!"

Grant entered the gallery and waltzed up the stairs.

That cocky smile of his. I could have kicked his fucking head in.

Gumby was sitting near the copier when he sat down to write.

If he did it again we will have him banged up for life.

We were through the back door before you could say *Jumping Jack Flash*.

*Webster* hauled the evil bastard down to the car.

Vicky put the handcuffs on and we drove him out to the sticks.

The tape was running:

Name: V. A. Grant. DOB 2/2/1946.

DI Roberts and DI Cuthbertson present.

"What were you doing on the 3rd Jan. What do you mean you were spending some book tokens? The description fits you down the ground."

"You are a MAP 3 and you always will be."

"You might as well admit it was you!"

Complaints had been logged and evidence gathered. He was always going to be in the frame. You can catch a thief but you can never catch a pathological storyteller.

Now that we have you on the Register you will be subject to unscheduled visits for the rest of your frigging days.

I hit the magic recall button.

I drool over these amazing SOPO's. Quickest route back inside and no nonsense. We use them against anyone we don't like and that includes the B.N.P.

I always look forward to my private chin wags with the Editor: £/$.

Grant! The days when you can go freely about your business are speeding rapidly to a close.

You know what!

The cheeky bastard insisted he had *simply forgotten to log-out at the local library*, and that another service user must have used his ID on-line.

We will find a way. No matter what the cost.

There will be many more opportunities to run him in before we reach a successful conclusion.

## I spoke to the Judge

**I spoke to the Judge at Norwich County Court today. Wherry had tried to pull another fast one along with their** friends down at the station. He adjourned the trial until another date could be arranged because he was not prepared to go ahead without a key witness.
Your Honour! I shouldn't even be there.
I haven't done anything wrong.
Not that innocence has ever bothered an Officer of the Law.

# THOUGHT MACHINE

-

By Hazel Hepplewhite

-

## Act 1

## Scene i

*Music - The Script – 'Hall of fame.'*

The four Executives of the Committee enter and find a seat.

The COMMISSIONER (*in uniform*) takes off his hat.

RUNCIE (*wearing dog-collar*) positions a chair for the HOME SECRETARY.

TINDALL stubs his cigarette out on the carpet.

ANTIPOV:     Ladies and gentlemen, Commissioner, Home Secretary, I would like to introduce to you the world's first thought reading machine.  The finest creation ever invented.

This *revelation* has been an *inspiration* (he nods to RUNCIE).  In the *right hands* it will transform out of all recognition the world in which we live.

(*A sigh of satisfaction from the COMMISSIONER*).

For the first time in history we will be able to know exactly what someone is going to do before they do it.

Long years of careful research into brain waves have resulted in the Ray-gun you see before you today.

By pointing the beam directly at a chosen target and pressing the light trigger a stream of gamma rays collides with their

Neuro-transmitters, producing a chemical reaction in the frontal lobe adjacent to the cerebral cortex.

The reading given on the counter is deciphered at once into thought patterns to produce an accurate interpretation of the target's intentions.  By matching this to activity in the subconscious domain we can comprehend the culprit's intended movements with absolute accuracy.  Infallible! Yes I would say so.  My name: Howard Antipov.

I have patented the Ray-gun under the name of *'Disaster-master.'*

On my way here I just happened to see a bank holdup.

By pointing my Ray-gun at the temples of the gunman I was rapidly able to discover that he was about to shoot the cashier straight through the chest and empty his cartridge into the surrounding onlookers.  A fact which became clear only moments later.

The Machine is able to decipher thoughts directly from the unconscious even before the suspect is aware of their own intentions.

*Gasps.  Muttering among the audience.*

COMMISIONER (*Turning to the side*): I like the sound of that!

RUNCIE:  Thinking is just as bad as doing.

TINDALL:  What kind of materials were used in its construction?

ANTIPOV:  We used a light metal alloy for the fixed body and the kinetic fields were constructed from depleted uranium shells.

TINDALL:  Could there be any residual effect on the target.  Is there any possibility the waves would interfere with a culprit's intended motion?

ANTIPOV:  I can test this for you immediately (*shaking his head*). *He takes it out of its box (its phallic shaped).*
*(He points the thought machine directly at TINDALL). It makes a MOO sound like a cow.*
*(Sniggers from the HOME SECRETARY).*
*(COMMISIONER laughing into his hand).*

COMMISSIONER: (*shrugs*) *(Holds his hands out as if pretending to throttle someone).*
*He sneezes, and as he reaches into his pocket for his hanky a pair of handcuffs fall to the floor.*

HOME SECRETARY:  How soon could you go into production?

ANTIPOV:  We have two hundred machines already waiting to be cleared.  I can have a thousand units delivered to every precinct in the country before the next act of civil disobedience.
We have seventy of our brightest technicians in the think-tank laboratory to thank for their unstinting efforts.
I would like to see the day when the *deterrent* will become our biggest earning export (*mopping his brow*).

RUNCIE:  I'm as randy as a Billy-goat in a paddy field.

COMMISIONER (jerks his head): Could you run through how we use the hand-lever.  I'm dying to have a go myself, aren't you? (To TINDALL).

HOME SECRETARY: I'm loving it already. What do you say to that Commissioner Begum? Best news we've had since the delivery of the new water cannon…

COMMISSIONER:  I'm in favour.  Thank you Home Secretary.

RUNCIE:  I'll second that!

COMMISSIONER:  I'm all for it.

HOME SECRETARY:  Gross indecency.   Can't wait to hear more.

TINDALL (muttering):  Shift the burden of responsibility...

RUNCIE:  Insider.

ANTIPOV:  And the head-guard is made from a specially coated titanium compound to protect the user.

We are confident that we can predict the intentions of a target at least twenty years prior to the event.

A new team of experts are working flat out to see if we can reach back as far as birth.

COMMISIONER: Wow! (the COMMISIONER and HOME SECRETARY both turn to look at each other).

HOME SECRETARY:  I can see tremendous rewards in this.  Possibly a knighthood.

COMMISSIONER:  I'm liking this more and more.

ANTIPOV:  They could retail for around half a million.

HOME SECRETARY:  Cheap at the price.

RUNCIE:  An end to crime.

HOME SECRETARY (To COMMISSIONER):   We'd have to introduce a new law banning them from sale to the general public of course.

RUNCIE:  Tough on crime, and tough on the causes of crime!

COMMISSIONER:  At last we will be able to castrate the flasher before he rapes his victim.

ANTIPOV (*laughing hysterically*):   Apprehend the psychopathic stalker before they go on to bludgeon their victim to death.

HOME SECRETARY:  We could jail the speeding motorist before they even get in the car.

COMMISSIONER:  Sentence the fraudster before they fill out their tax return.

TINDALL:  You could.

RUNCIE:  We could have one of these contraptions on every parish council in the county.

I'd like to see it in every main stream school as soon as possible.

HOME SECRETARY:  I'm sure of that.

# Scene ii

-

## **Darkness.**

*ANTIPOV in Judge's wig skulking across the room with his invention.*

*Playing around with a toy sword.*

*Packing it into his suitcase.*

*Counting his money (spitting into his hands).*

*Fiddling with his zipper.*

*Tampering with the levers.*

*Moaning and cursing.*

*Flapping his arms like a bat.*

# Scene iii

*Enter: the four members of the Committee:*

HOME SECRETARY has a small Chihuahua dog with her on a lead.

*They find a seat at the front: the COMMISSIONER takes off his hat.  RUNCIE moves a chair out for the HOME SECRETARY (he is also carrying a missal).*

*TINDALL stubs his cigarette out under his foot.*

*BEARDED MAN is dragged in by two heavily protected OFFICERS.*

*ANTIPOV hands them his print-out.  He holds his invention aloft for everyone to admire.*

ANTIPOV:   As guilty as a sex-fiend in a nunnery!

BEARDED MAN:  I didn't do anything.

RUNCIE:  Well I never....tut tut (*makes a circular movement with his finger at the side of his head*).

TINDALL (*turns to the COMMISSIONER with notepad in hand*):
(*Mutters*)  A menace to society?

BEARDED MAN:  A public menace!

COMMISSIONER (*whispers something in TINDALL'S ear*).

TINDALL: Tell me later Commissioner.

HOME SECRETARY: A classic case of cognitive distortion and a total lack of social responsibility.

RUNCIE:  Moral fibre!

BEARDED MAN:  I never lifted a finger.

HOME SECRETARY: The machine seems to be leaking fuel....?

TINDALL: (laughs).

COMMISSIONER:  Brought to Justice.

HOME SECRETARY:   I'm sure of that.

RUNCIE:  A dereliction of duty.  A total lack of something which he needs.

ANTIPOV: The offender was observed dropping litter in the street and chased across the city by a squadron of panda-cars. The *public protection unit* were alerted and a search of his home made on the spot. A knife was found lying upon a draining board in the kitchen. The light beam was directed into his eyes and a reading taken from the *mind-o-meter*.

RUNCIE: Guilty as charged: a litter-bug!

COMMISSIONER: Now we have him!

HOME SECRETARY: Whatever next!

Thank goodness. (To *COMMISSIONER*) What do you think of the new uniforms?

RUNCIE: Glory be to god in the most high place of correction.

HOME SECRETARY: Before he could do anything more.

COMMISSIONER: Subvert the course of Justice!

TINDALL: (*swiftly taking down notes*).

ANTIPOV: The reading clearly reveals that the delinquent was about to do something *extremely wicked*.

COMMISSIONER: Anything could have happened. A member of the security forces could have been sprayed with pepper. We apprehended the villain just in time then?

RUNCIE: Well, bless my soul.

HOME SECRETARY (to *BEARDED MAN*): You'll be taken away and shot!

TINDALL: Not without beating him to pulp first I hope?

RUNCIE (*To BEARDED MAN*): It's for your own good.

BEARDED MAN (begins kissing the feet of RUNCIE).
Thank you! How long have I got?

RUNCIE: Not long. I wouldn't start writing your memoirs (*chuckles*).

HOME SECRETARY: I like the sound of that.

COMMISSIONER: Had it coming to him for a long time.

HOME SECRETARY: I'm sure of that.

TINDALL:  Jobs a good 'un.


HOME SECRETARY:  Handled in the most appropriate manner possible.


*BEARDED MAN (dragged away in handcuffs).*


The End


## QUESTIONS TO MR YAHMAN

May I ask you:

1 Why has Bure Valley Zoo got such a bad reputation in the town? That's one thing you can't blame on me? When the trouble first started and I asked to speak to you about Christine being bullied why did you refuse to speak to me even though you were there when I rang?

2 Do you believe it's true that I have been going around tapping on windows and trying to get into someone's flat at night?

3 Are there any cameras at Bure Valley Shithouse or in the Car Park? How are you always able to know when I am there?

4 How come you know so much about everyone?

5 Its stated that Mrs Didwell handed over sixty of her diaries which contained notes about my behaviour. What is the total number of diaries she has done for you. Could we have them here so we can take a look at some of them please?

6 How many times has Christine Didwell and Vera Temple rang you about me (I was passing Vera Temple's room one day and heard her say she was going to ring you about me being in the garden as soon as you got in Monday morning: "Trust me. I'll lay it on really thick!").

7 Do you *seriously* believe that we openly had sex in the garden or that we have banged repeatedly on the wall for hours?

8 I do apologise for losing my cool when you called at my mother's house with the police to give me the new injunction. I really let myself down but I am so sick of being hounded by you and by your attempts to embarrass me in front of my new neighbours. As I told you then: the First Injunction was based on lies and I felt you were harassing me again even though I left Bure Valley months ago.

9 What do you think about 'malicious reporting.' Do you think malicious reporting is a form of 'harassment?' Why have you never done anything to stop this form of harassment?

11 After I moved out in April can you confirm that you threatened me with a hefty fine unless I removed a few items I'd left behind?

12 Why have you never done anything to stop the harassment of Mrs Pigott by her neighbour? What did you do to stop the abuse against her by some of her neighbours? What did you think of some of the slanderous remarks made by people such as Didwell and Temple (SHAP rep) against myself and Mrs Pigott. What did you do to stop them?

13 True or false. You are determined to label me as a *nasty dangerous neighbour* even though I moved away from BVH months ago. What have you got against me. How are your friends down at the station by the way?

### Questions to Bully Bryant

1 Why did you tell Christine that she would lose her home unless she split up with me?

2 Is it you who has been going around saying I scratched your car? What evidence do you have apart from gossip, malicious gossip and a determination to spread rumours?

3 You don't like me do you. Has this got anything to do with the things which have been said about me before we actually met?

4 You've been at BVH how long? How is the 'moral well being' of Residents going to be improved by my departure? Are you saying that I am 'immoral?'

5 Has Temple or Didwell ever been in the office to tell tales about me and how often. Every morning, like they did when the previous Support Manager was there?

6 From the first moment you started you were always picking on me about petty little things. Didn't you ever get tired of knocking on my door as soon as you got to work?

7 Why have you been going around saying I am banned from the building for the last few months?

8 Do you always believe the word of Fatass?

9 Do you truly believe that I am responsible for knocking on the doors and windows late at night and for the bearded lady's mental health?

10 Why have you been deliberately promoting the idea I am dangerous and aggressive? Isn't this based on your own prejudices from the very start.

11 Seven months ago while I was moving some things out of my old flat you ordered me to smash up a perfectly decent wardrobe which would have been useful to someone and place it in the skip.

You also ordered me to dispose of some other items which someone could have had. ie personal care products, cups and plates etc.

12 Much of your statement is deliberate scare-mongering. I had two helpers with me while removing these things. I put it to you that your attitude is based on prejudice and that no Resident was ever in any danger of harm from me as you implied in your Statement.

13 I put it to you that it is your attitude and your friend's attitude which is the problem. Your assumption that the atmosphere at BVH has improved since I went is all down to your imagination. I suggest that your assertion that Residents are in fear of me is down to gossip, malicious gossip and information being leaked from your office (of which I made several complaints when I was there).

I have never harmed anyone at BVH and never would. I put it to you that you were biased against me from the very beginning and that you have colluded in this witch-hunt against me.

COMMENTS

## Finding Genevieve

The first time I tried to get rid of Genevieve was on Morecambe beach in 1963.

We'd had it with the donkey rides and were bored with making sand castles. My father had lain out in the sun for longer than was good for him, and had emptied a large crate of Newcastle Brown. My mother had taken us for a paddle in the sea. It was freezing cold, but what do you expect at one of our countries leading holiday resorts in August···

Our parents decided to leave for the car. A grey Morris 1100, with red leather seats and a travelling bowl for Genevieve.

The strand looked like a leap of lobsters. I glared back to see my little sister still playing obliviously in the sand. I knew she hadn't heard them call her. I tagged along behind them, taking an occasional glance back to see if she was following, hurrying them along, hoping they wouldn't notice. It wasn't until we reached the end of the beach and were about to climb over the railings that I heard my mother's frantic calls. They searched all over the place but they still couldn't find her. We returned to the sand castles which were now a mess of mud, and found her spade. After two desperate hours we went to the Pen-for-lost-children. She was knelt huddled in the middle of the square looking miserable and forlorn. Her dress was grubby and she'd lost her ice-cream. When she saw us she got up from the floor and scuttled across the tarmac. I've never seen my dad look so relieved.

It was her cold feet I didn't like, and anyway, why should she be the only one allowed to stay? Why should she be the only one who could have a birthday party or give hugs to the head of the family? I was constantly being ordered to find somewhere else to live and I didn't know why. I began to wonder what I had done to upset him. At night we hid under the sheets. It wasn't that we were scared of the dark. But we were aware of the time···

I escorted her down to the bus-stop one day. You could see it from our kitchen window. I read the bus-timetable to her. I'd given her all my pocket money. I only knew she didn't belong with us···

"All you have to do is get on the bus!" I said. "You can go wherever you like. Just ask the driver."

A few months later Doctor Brogden came to take a swab from us at home. My sister was identified as a diphtheria 'carrier' and had to be quarantined for the next six weeks at St Luke's Hospital.

I had the place to myself.

I rejoiced in my deliverance.

I loved seeing her and Margaret Stowell behind the ward window.

A rumour began to circulate that something really terrible had happened.  Spellis said that two girls from Miss Bergen's class had gone to the Confessional in church at lunchtime.  A man wearing a dark suit and dog collar had left his side of the grill and exited the booth.  Then he went into *our side.* We heard about it only in whispers.  One of the girls never returned.  The other one was treated like a *Cliff Richard.* I'm not sure if he was ever caught.

My father was reduced to parking his car outside our school and waiting for the alarm bell to ring.  My mum had finally decided to throw in the towel after he broke down the door.

In 1966 Mr Eardley had just got married and my sister was in his class.  He stood at our classroom door looking rather sad.  I wasn't sure if I could make it through the day myself.  Had I done something wrong?  Had Lynch been caught drinking the paint water again?

I was asked to go down the stairs to his classroom to sit with my sister next to her desk.  St Anne's was a maze of corridors. It would have been easy to lose your way.

"Can you help," he said.  "Do you think you can do anything with her?"

I had to remain there for *over an hour.*

I kept hearing stories about Genevieve waiting at the school gate and going outside.  I don't know what her idea was but it sounded bloody crazy to me.  There were a lot of fast cars on North Street and an old Gas works. On a plinth above the entrance stood a statue of the Virgin Mary.

Canon Holdright said that we lived in the best country in the world, and that we all had a Guardian angel. He said that even people from our school could sometimes stray from the path.

A couple of weeks later she disappeared completely, and it was almost bonfire night.  The police were called and a search was made of the whole area.  They searched the local park, the Railway station, the nearby streets, and the canal. I imagined her lost somewhere among the town's dark satanic mills, or even worse, trapped in Mr Atkinson's greenhouse. I felt sure she must be somewhere at the bottom of Alum pot or Gaping Gill.  She'd been spotted wandering around in the rain.  Even Fisher came up to talk to me.

Eventually she was found walking up the road to our old house:  "just looking for daddy."

I couldn't help feeling that all my plans had been scuppered, and that her return would disrupt the cosy relationship I had nurtured with my mother. That Sunday my father moaned all day about my sister's absence.  A deep frown burrowed into his forehead. I felt as if I had let him down somehow. Personally, I thought that *hiking in the Yorkshire Dales* was a perfectly valid excuse for her to go away and never come back.

On the hill where we played Genevieve was always somewhere just behind me.  She hounded me wherever I went.  We laked around all summer in the fields, with Jeannie, and Neil and Margaret Beverage. There was a wood nearby with a stone trough in its shadow. We took our jam-jars along to collect tadpoles and hunt for blackberries. That was when a day seemed to crawl along like a turtle.

The fields above the Railway line and the Water towers.

That's where we collected our sunlight.

That's where you could see all the toxic waste and heavy-industry.

The Estate where we went to live deployed an army of emaciated and ravenous greyhounds. I hung my head in shame if anyone asked me where I lived. Someone threw a banger through our letterbox. Waste bins sent scraps of paper floating all over the streets. Widows and reprobates peered from behind a crop of tea stained curtains. If you left your pushbike up against a wall for longer than five minutes it was sprayed a different colour and you saw another kid riding it. My mother became the centre of a tide of abuse because she worked for the Department of Employment. There were young women in *summer clothes* gathered at every street corner, peering expectantly from side to side. I was still playing with my electric train-set and collecting postage stamps.

My sister gained a scholarship to the new convent school in Bradford. She passed her eleven-plus with flying colours. On her way home from school one day she was approached by a stranger who claimed he was an Officer-of-the-law. At the age of twelve she went walking across a field with a man I didn't know and that's when I lost her forever···just after my father took his own life.

I was seventeen and still blushed if anyone looked at me. When she said she was leaving home I felt a lump in my throat. She was always *stopping at her friend's house* at the weekend: I didn't look old enough to get in a night-club myself even though I was one year older.

It wasn't until six months after it *took place* that my mum told me we had nearly lost our Genevieve. She had been carrying Steve's baby when he ran off with another woman and she'd taken a huge overdose of barbiturates. I'd been coming home late one night when he paid me back for letting the cat out of the bag.

It felt like I had gone through the wrong front door and ended up in hell. I was sent to see the Headmaster for missing school. How I avoided being sent to the loony bin is completely beyond me. Consigned to oblivion I drifted from one lousy job to another. My whole life seemed to have gone down the plughole.

In 1985 my sister emigrated to Canada where she taught drama and managed to escape her husband. I didn't see or hear from her for years. I suspect it was her children she was trying to protect. She left me a store of books under the bed: '*the Book thief, the Tin drum, All you need to know about Catholics.*' I heard on the news that she was in New York, Jerusalem, and Iran. Not a single postcard. Not a single phone call. Surely he couldn't have been as bad as all that.

I was sitting quietly at table number six. I could see other tables like mine all around the hall. They ordered me to wear an orange vest. They told me I had to wear jeans and a blue striped shirt.   Strangers scowled at me across the floor. I suppose we can all get to the stage where you want to end it all.

My sister has been living in Monaghan for over twenty years.  She wanted to make a fresh start. To put it all behind her.  To forget she even had a brother. They say my father was buried in the cemetery there.  They say that.  Who am I to say?

The Guard came to stand beside me:  "Stay right where you are!"  he growled.

I could see a very slim middle-aged woman enter through the far door. She looked fearful. She looked as if she shouldn't be there... Genevieve had been receiving treatment for throat cancer. I'd last seen her at Uncle Tommy's funeral, when a wasp had stung her toe, and that was a long time ago. I hardly recognised her.  She'd been frisked from top to bottom.  I don't think she was very used to it.

The Guard leant a little closer as she approached and dusted his lapel.

Genevieve quivered beside me.  I stood up and embraced my little sister. That's when she began to cry.

# What I would do to cyclists who jump red lights

I was slowing down approaching the traffic lights when someone flew past my wing mirror.

He clipped the edge, but didn't stop.  I watched the cyclist go whizzing across the lights, nearly colliding with a pedestrian, who had somehow got trapped on the kerb.

The zebra crossing was full of rush-hour students.

When the lights turned to green I ambled patiently past Barclay's.

It was slow progress down London road towards Headington Hill.

Then I saw him again, racing the other way.

The Scoundrel mounted the pavement  a second time sending onlookers diving into the wall.

He went speeding towards the shops.

By the time I reached the second set of lights I saw him plummeting towards me again in my cab mirror.

It was the same guy.  Blue specs. Air Jordans. Bald as an Auschwitz inmate.

He seemed to slow down, then he darted through the lights again.

The road was heaving with traffic.  A bus had broken down on the opposite side.

It was a steep descent.  The cyclist tore down the hill.  I could see him streaking away in the distance.

His orange kagoule rattled like a windy tent.

The lights at the bottom of the hill were clearly at red.  The traffic was jam-packed on either side.

Another line of motorists waited to the left.

Just as the lights began to change I saw him brake, and then shoot out in front of all the traffic.

A truck carrying several tractors from the nearby motor plant desperately papped it's horn, but it was too late.  The cyclist skidded under its front wheel and was crushed to death.

I saw the paramedics arrive and try to resuscitate him, but it was clearly a waste of time.

I saw several motorists burst out laughing.  I could hardly wipe the smile off my face.

# The Swirling

We did not come in dark clouds,
but billowing in the fury of ships,
disturbed the slumber of the Sun,
brandishing Bran's flame.
We burnt the decks-of-wood,
Our words like hidden conifers,
leading us to the land.
Where the fair and emerald,
rich in seeds:
Sword of light,
giver of life,
Stone of Fall,
spear of Lugh.
Vanquished:
the formidable Fir Bolg,
Banba Eire Fodla.
We stood on the beautiful ridge,
knowing each hill,
each blade,
every kilt and pulsing wave,
were woven with our daylight spells.
Three days and nights,
laid in the house,
Banba Eire Fodla,
until defeated we shrank,
backwards,
into the dew-deep soil.

# BELINDA'S HOT AIR

(a place to pour scorn on the world)

## Current topics of interest:

**Bashir al-Assad**    **How to direct laser beams at aircraft**    **Badger cull**

**Argon chambers**    **Acid attack**

**The French Royal family**    **Putin to marry Kate Moss**


# Dip Your Wick

*'Human interference has imposed spiteful laws, so that jealous regulations forbid what nature itself allows'*

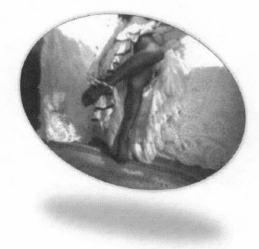

# At four in the morning

At four in the morning,
should I stay for good,
or be on my way...
The morning kettle hot,
Against my touch,
And two purple beakers,
Specially ground,
with coffee.
I climb the stairs,
Spilling a drop...
A simple task before I leave...
The smell of sugar-cane,
Written in the book of sleep.
First Emily x
Then Benji x
Then Mummy x


# Red-hat day

Today is red-hat day,
it's a Thursday,
and you know,
what that means.


# Return of the blue Cannondale

An old friend is meeting me at the gate,
The one I have nightmares about,
Losing.
It's the one I went on-the-run with,
Which was hunted all over the country.
The one she so admired,
on the road to Luqa.

# 'Inappropriate' sexual references

By <u>Bird Dung</u> | Published: October 17, 2015 | <u>Edit</u>

## Says who?

## <u>Acid attack</u>

By <u>Peter Smith</u> | Published: October 16, 2015 | <u>Edit</u>

The number of acid attacks has been rising slowly since the banning of saw-off shotguns and kitchen knives.  If the State says it is wrong to seek revenge then it must be.

*There will always be plenty more to take your place!*

# *The right to offend*

By <u>Rumplestiltskin</u> | Published: October 17, 2015 | <u>Edit</u>

The right to offend is always more important than the right not to be offended.  Otherwise that would be the end of free speech and we would all be living in a fascist dictatorship?

# COMMENTS

# MOUNTAIN CLIMBING

For five years my mountain climbing had been in the doldrums.
I have scarcely climbed a single solitary peak. By September
however I was ready to climb again and felt the blood throbbing
once more in my veins.  I find that a sturdy pair of boots helps
in this sort of recreation... I like the fur-topped variety and the
insides warm against my skin..

We began our ascent in the early hours of the morning and
continued on till lunchtime, passing the high firs and the snow-
line beneath us.  My own part in this most favoured of activities
is beyond dispute. We celebrated each crest with a loud fanfare
of cheering and jubilation.

The air was sharp and the sun-like radiator hot against my
touch.  Like all great enterprises it is really a matter of peaks
and troughs, a gentle and persistent rising of the heart.

A series of challenges leading us to a higher plain.

I accept my responsibilities with the tenacity of snow-leopard.
(We sometimes have to catch our breath before ploughing on
again into the clouds). We opened our lungs with bramble and
lace.  I'm lagging behind somewhat. It's par for the course.

Together we troop through the mist, the crystalline passion of
life.  It's seven, then we take stock.

Another peak beckons breast-high in the distance.

"More, more, more!" she screams over the heat of the col.

We like to make our journeys unplanned.

A serendipitous adventure. A ferocious dipping of tongues.

There's not much she doesn't know about rock-climbing.

I'm slow to ascend. I begin my descent.

Confucius

# Eric Heiffer's gorgeous pink urinals -

by Hazel Hepplewhite

I've nothing against psychopaths. I just don't want any of them living
next door to my daughter. After one of them went on the rampage in
my home town I was determined to find a way to sniff them out before
it ever happened again. I began my study in the middle of August.
We had just finished our Annual Conference. The Seniors all swarmed
out of the Conference room with a self satisfied gleam. I walked
down the corridor and entered my office. My desk was covered in
newspaper cuttings. I had my family photo on top for everyone to
see. A few carefully chosen books stood alongside. You could never
point the finger at me for being superficial, or even flippant, for that
matter. My partner suffers from acute anxiety straightening my tie: it's
the people I have to work with. I shed a tear each time I lock up my
four wheel drive.
The Receptionist called me at half past three. I composed myself. I
drank a glass of water. I belched. The reprobate arrived bang on time.
His silhouette loomed ominously in the door panel. I finished dusting
my picture and wiping the mist from its glass.
"Enter!"
I'd only just managed to get him ahead of Jenkins. He opened the
door and closed it behind him. I gestured warmly towards the tiny
infant chair. No-one is ever going to accuse me of being impolite or of
namby pamby airs and graces.
"Take a seat Mr. Sceitel. Did you have a pleasant journey? Let's begin
by introducing ourselves."
"My name is Mandy Webster, and I am going to be your New
Treatment Manager."
I have always liked the sound of that. It made me want to kiss my own ass.
"A completely blank canvas...!" I said.
Sceitel perched on the pink cushion looking a little puzzled. His face
was like a ripe tomato and he was puffing like a steam engine. There
were grease marks on his collar and his forehead perspired like a
condensed windowpane. I shook my head and glanced down at the
label on his footwear. I opened my note pad and stared with horror at
his file. Inside the cover lay a fair to passing resemblance.

'DANGEROUS TO ALL LIVING CREATURES'

I thought that an accurate summary of his overall potential.

"Would you like to tell me anything about your earliest years? Everything you say will be completely confidential."

He shrugged his shoulders and began mumbling under his breath.

"Did you say 'cellar?'"

He glared out of the window.

I rubber stamped my pad with:

CHILDHOOD TRAUMA

And gave him my rattlesnake stare.

I scribbled intently. I ticked the box. This was obviously going to be a very difficult time for me. I must learn to take things steady.

"Aren't people wonderful?" I said.

People are wonderful!"

Sceitel jerked his head and removed his dark glasses. He was wearing some beige corduroys with a bare patch on the knees. I was sure I could smell dope.

"You know that smoking is against the rules?"

I circled the words 'Control AND Restraint' and...

RISK TAKER

"Some of us have to work for a living!" I snarled.

He looked up at the ceiling.

"As the Gestapo Officer said to the trembling shower hose."

I gave him my extremely wounded expression.

His skin was pale. Stuck to his chin were a few random ginger threads. I took a walnut from the bowl and crushed it with my hard to medium crackers. Got on the phone to his shrink.

"How long have you been in residence at the Elms?"

The Elms was opened in the early 60's by his Lordship the Duke as a secure unit for the criminally insane.

Sceitel had been with us for seven years, and I would dare lay all the money I have he would be with us for seven more. I am going to make damn sure he never gets out if he continues to chew gum during our meetings.

We began our picture show. I offered him a toffee. I did not waver from my mission. I played my ace. Do-gooders have a lot on their plates: life is just a big fat slob waiting to be cured of a compulsion to eat. There's nothing we can't do if we put our minds to it. On the screen before us a parade of the most offensive and shocking images we could find lit up the whole room. He laughed them off with a strange cheerful exuberance. He said that he'd seen worse things on the streets of Kosovo.

"Cool!"

'Inappropriate,' I wrote,' highly inappropriate.' Not a chance in hell!

"You do know that all human life is precious!"

"What do you mean, why?"

"What kind of idiotic reply is that, Sceitel?"

"You would argue the sky was pink just for the sake of it..." I beamed.

# IRINA GAIDAMACHUK

"The bitch!" he said.

"I hope you aren't referring to Miss Woodbridge? Don't let me hear you use that disgusting word again!"

He explained that he was only describing a normal animal behaviour.

I flicked open the daily log and wrote: 'No flies on Sceitel.' Not yet anyhow.

There were times when I wanted to shout and scream and poke him in the eye, but I just managed to contain myself. He could be as superficially charming as he liked it wasn't going to make a scrap of difference.

"Any ambitions?"

"Any inhibitions?"

"I'm going to be a future winner of the Bridport Prize!"

What a cunt!

"With your carry on?"

Not while you have a hole in your back end mate:

DELUSIONS OF GRANDEUR

The little shit-head. A bad attitude. A wrong attitude, totally unemployable.

"You have a wrong attitude, sonny!"

Of course violence is wrong.

Scietel disagreed. Big surprise, eh?

He laid out his plans to bring about a reduction in the planet's population.

I was horrified by what he suggested. "You're mad!" I said. "You should be locked up..."

"And anyway, there is no exit gate for the lions!"

What do you expect from a Sociopath. A delinquent like him. Said we were vastly over rated. Who he was referring to, I don't know. A former member of the S.A.S. Everyone knows it's wrong to hit back.

"You know it's wrong! I don't want to hear any more of your silly excuses!"

Sceitel said he would like to train as a Clinical Psychologist. His father worked from the back of a fruit lorry and I think this would have suited him perfectly well too.

Suddenly there was a knock at the door. My fellow professional whispered outside the room.

"Use your buzzer if you have to. I will only be next door."

I returned to my desk and scribbled: '*Predictor of future behaviour.*' UNDERLINE.

"Shall we agree to differ on this?" I placed my receiver considerately back on its stand.

He signed his appointment card with the same cocky grin and slid out of the exit.

"That's it. Fuck off back to your lonely miserable padded cell," I muttered. "And have a very solitary old age!"

I asked Sceitel about his parents. What made him go to the gun cupboard that morning? Why had he refused to wear his green jacket into the garden? Sceitel said he had worshipped both his parents.

I suspect he was being somewhat disingenuous. I noticed a smirk spread across his face.

We had just received the results of his eighth set of 'preliminary' tests.

These psychometrics are the most valuable tool we have in assessing the pathology of a client.

I was not at all astounded how often the scores actually increased. Psychopaths are very devious as we know. I have known many of them to fake their tests and to have deliberately thwarted any attempt to gain an insight into their warped and twisted ways of interpreting reality.

I glanced at his file: LIKES: Rap.

"So, you are you a Rapper?"

"Dizzee Rascal?"

My over-burdened work colleague returned a moment later. He was interviewing the very lowest of the low. We call them 'the scum of the earth:' a Sex-Offender. Poor old Jenkins! I hope he washes his hands. We spoke outside the room again.

Sceitel was casually reading a magazine.

When I returned he was standing up and putting on his coat.

"I'll have that, before you go!"

We need to check for any rude words in our private library.

After he left I tidied up my desk.

Simpson was in the next cubicle when I sat down for a fag.
I pushed the file under the cubicle wall. Another confidential file
appeared for me to read which had me in stitches.
"He never did!"
Simpson cracked on the wall and I reached for the bog roll.
Sceitel's file lay in a quagmire beneath me.
I smudged the print and added ...ing large Termites.
At our next meeting I discovered that 'Skell' suffered from a rare eating
disorder.  I was determined to link this to his illness. And he is very ill.
There's no denying that.
He listed the atrocities committed on behalf of legally elected
governments.
"Unlike arseholes like you they acted completely within the law. You
do have some very odd ways of thinking."
He stretched, he yawned, and he scratched underneath his armpits.
I questioned him about his relationship with his father. He declined to
answer. I was forced to record this as a REFUSAL.
What do you expect from someone at the higher end of the
spectrum?
I asked if it was his mother who dealt with discipline within the family
home. He was being evasive. As we know:
ALL PSYCHOPATHS ARE PATHOLOGICAL LIARS
They are lightning swift in their responses and can make up a whole
host of plausible answers in no time. We can get them sectioned so
fast their feet don't even touch the ground. I must speak to Marian
about her Summer's party...
Sceitel stared at me from the dismal regions of his pink coloured stool.
'I will prove the link between your behaviour and Dutch Emmental if it's
the last thing I do!'
"No-one's going to put words into your mouth. Or anything else for
that matter!"
I sometimes feel like a Catholic priest about to hear confession.
"Give a dog a bad name!" he faltered.
He peered down at his bootlace. I looked at my wrist.
His bootlaces seemed unusually long. I started to frown.
I began to loosen my tie and sweat a little.
 "Do you ever regret any of your actions?"
"Remorse of conscience is indecent!"

"So you don't think you did anything *wrong*?"

"Wrong is just a point of view..."

An erroneous school of thought. He'll come a cropper one of these days with an attitude like that! The clever prick.

I was there when they found Jenkins's body under the stairs. It was lying face-down in a waste paper bin near the fire escape. We called the ambulance just as Sceitel was passing the pool on his lawn mower. I'm going to make damn sure he doesn't get any more protein powder. Try smirking this one off, you asshole!

'*There isn't a stone you can crawl under where the right won't find You!*'

I played him the tapes and made him look at the disturbing images from my computer. I, of course, was immune from their contamination. Jenkin's body was covered in ink marks. We couldn't find his biro. We still can't find his biro!

I gazed across the table at Scietel, who was making a ring with his hair.

"Do you think your brain is wired up the *wrong* way?"

He quoted the incident of a British soldier given a medal of honour for gallantry. He had the bloody gall to imply that our marvellous Royal family had gained their position by very similar means.

I took him by the ear down to the fingerprint lab and had him sit for an hour. I used my throw-away to take his hideous mug shot. Say cheese you evil bastard!

"You have grown a beard. If you grow your hair too long we will have to drag you down there again."

"This is your FINAL WARNING!"

" You just drift around the village without any true sense of moral purpose..."

"Get your feet down from my desk!"

"So, am I suffering from an abnormal psychopathic disorder?" he grins.

"Teach a lesson....teach who a lesson?" I asked.

You don't need to be an expert in psychoneurosis to understand that anyone who speaks like that needs a long course of Electro convulsive shock-therapy. And that is just what I am going to recommend at our next monthly meeting.

 "I suppose a full-frontal lobotomy is out of the question?"

The cheeky git!

"You know what will happen if you forget to take all your medication?"

I jangled the keys above my head and began making some more exploratory notes.

He gaped at me like a hungry puppy dog.

I spoke to Jenny in the office.

"Worse case of brain rot I've ever come across."

"Wanted to celebrate the life of Jimmy one thing or another."

Jenkins would have laughed his balls off.

"He won't do what he's fucking well told!"

"Are you a good man, or a bad man?" I asked.

The stupid little fucker didn't even know which one he was!

"He held up a picture in either hand. You pick. Who do you think always told the truth?"

"I'm not here to judge a popularity contest. I'm here to make damn sure you don't escape!"

"Total lack of empathy. Never showed a grain of remorse for anything he'd done."

Kept asking 'Why?'

Huh?

A maladjusted dreck of ass wipes!

That's when I closed my drawer and locked the office safe.

"Have the common decency," I said.


I always look forward to the weekends when I can 'Punk-Up.'

Like every well meaning Good Samaritan I can lacquer my hair in pink and red.  I can shove my safety pin through my nostrils. I can rug munch Janet all day long if I have to.

I have a hunch he isn't telling me everything.

I found his attitude offensive.

"Discrimination?" he said. "Who could be more discriminated against than me?"

He was an 'Offender.'

His mere presence offended me.

The Secretary said he stared at her too.


We usually meet down at the station. We Probation staff. A London Derby: I tossed them a photo of Sceitel jerking off in the lav. Furness screamed like a donkey. We even have our cameras in their john.

Before long we were speeding through an urban grassland of canals and chemical waste. The debris of a confused and antagonistic industry. As rife as a leper colony.

Carmichael stuck her arse through the window. An intercity was speeding in the opposite direction.

She had a nice arse too.

Shortly after that we passed the cemetery where Jenkins had been
laid to rest.
"That's the spot!" blurted Grundledoper.
There was an immediate hush in the compartment. We all looked sadly
at each other.
Suddenly there was cheering. Just like on Cup final day when Adams
finally lifted the trophy.
We ripped out the seats and pissed in the corner.
'So what's in a name?' I said.
We'll call him a twat if we have to!

# Dear Alex,

Information is still being passed from Bure Valley Zoo to the police about me.
They were here harassing me again last week and had obviously been talking to
someone. Is there any way you could persuade Mehmet not to talk to them so often?  I told
them to go away and leave me alone because I hadn't done anything
wrong. At the Resident's meeting Louise went back on her word to offer us some
mediation. It was to appease the bullies who have been causing trouble.
They refused to go to any kind of mediation.  I was the only one to hold my hand
up or to talk in a positive way about where we live.  It gives the gang permission
to continue with their petty personal vendettas.

I decided to leave the meeting after Robert Lilly and Bert began to have words.
I thought it might diffuse the situation.

As we were leaving Robert used the 'c' word and was becoming more and more angry.
When I asked Jo in the office what she thought about the meeting a few minutes later she
rebuked me for using inappropriate language even though she must have known it was
Robert who swore.

Do you ever get the feeling this is all about 'labels?'

## Dear Job Centre, *NORMAN SCHWARZKOPF hive*

I have written this letter to help you understand why I have found it so hard to find employment. I hope it will help you to decide the best way forward. I have now completed the two year period with Seetec and have done everything they have asked me to do. Apart from two or three absences due to ill health I have attended all their appointments and actively sought work on each occasion. I followed their advice where it was offered. Overall they were very helpful and understanding. As a Manager at the Job Centre said: "All you can do is apply for work and one day someone might be willing to give you a chance. It's hardly likely, but you might as well give it a go."

I am still applying for work even though my health has deteriorated. I have not been well for nearly a year now and it is causing me grave concern. A few months ago I had a brain-scan because I had suddenly developed pains in the left side of my head. They were unable to pinpoint why I have been getting so many migraine headaches (they seem to occur on a regular basis about three days a week) but revealed that my brain had suffered some ischemic changes, due to lack of oxygen. When I get my headaches I usually feel extremely tired and sick. The only thing I can do is to rest in a quiet room until it goes off, but that can take more than twenty four hours. I will soon be in my sixtieth year. I last worked in 2007 when I acted as a Support Worker for a severely disabled person over in Oxfordshire. Everything came to a head when he died. I had been feeling very depressed for a long time and had tried to find some way of ending my life. I was in a relationship with someone but I wasn't happy. In fact I was depressed. I persuaded someone to send me a fire-arm on-line. It didn't actually work but I didn't throw it away. My relationship broke up because I couldn't make love to my girlfriend. I treated her with compassion the whole time I was there. I continued to keep in touch with her even though she sent me a few cruel messages and I was told not to. The police came round to see me and found the old firearm under the floor. I was given two years in prison and had to serve the full two years, for possession of a fire-arm without a certificate. While in prison I was attacked from behind by a very violent maniac. I was badly injured and had to be taken to hospital. When I came out of prison I was not allowed to have a normal life and had to sign at the desk every hour. I went out with a local businesswoman in Norfolk but was due to be recalled for coming back late from church and for walking her to her car one night, so I went on the run.

After I rang my ex-girlfriend on the phone to explain the misunderstanding I was re-arrested. The police dragged me from my car and beat me up at the side of the road. I suffered head injuries. In 2009 I was given a further two and a half years in prison for contacting my ex-partner on the phone (non threatening or malicious). This followed straight after the first sentence and I also had to serve the time I had spent 'at large.' During this time I was assaulted in the middle of the night by a male prisoner who was suffering from schizophrenia and suffered injuries to my face and head. I was released after half my sentence but was recalled after doing a Job Search on a computer at the Forum library without permission and for going on a Social Networking site. During this last period of incarceration I was assaulted by a group of inmates who tried to put my cell on fire and threw things at me…

After my release I was constantly harassed by the police and became homeless after the Manager of the hostel where I was living tried to evict me. She said that my probation period was over and that they were no longer funded to keep me. After a few months I was re-housed by Broadlands Council in a sheltered housing complex for odd people. I have been living there for the last two years. The police keep coming round all the time and are causing problems with my neighbours who think I'm some kind of sex fiend.

Before I arrived the police went round telling everyone I was a dangerous Sex-offender. My neighbours, along with the housing association, are trying to get rid of me because of my label. A long time ago I admitted one offence of 'exposure' when a female shop assistant saw me half undressed through a changing room curtain. I wrote the Manager a letter of apology. The police keep snooping through all my personal possessions and have informed me that if I don't open the door to them on each occasion they would get a search warrant, smash down my door and put me in prison for a further five years. I am suffering from severe anxiety and insomnia. When I first went to the Job Centre Security staff were told to stand over me all the time. This happens wherever I go. The police keep turning up where ever I go. I did try to do some voluntary work but they appeared on my first morning and told everyone I was a Sex-offender. On my final morning I had a bucket of water poured over me. I have tried to resettle close to my mother who is getting very frail. My stepfather died last year. She is worried that her friends and neighbours will hear about me and she will have to move. *Just over a year ago (with the aid of my partner Christine) I established a coffee/social morning where I am living at the old people's home. I have also managed to start a Writer's group in spite of opposition from the police. I recently applied for a job as a volunteer with 'Mind' but have not heard back from them even though they promised to respond. I cannot seem to relax or sleep at night even with pills. I am due to see the Doctor soon about another blood test. I have been suffering from more incontinence since my time in prison, numbness to my lips, hands and fingers. Lack of co-ordination. Pain in the extremities. Extreme exhaustion. Sickness and nausea. Forgetfulness and Jumbled handwriting. Fallen arches in foot. I've been diagnosed with arthritis in both legs. The 'Restrictions' imposed on me by the police (i.e. prevented from talking to anyone under eighteen years of age) are making it very difficult for me to have a normal life. I have written to numerous Solicitors for help but none of them ever reply.

I have had my claims of harassment upheld by the IPCC but nothing was ever done. I am suffering from stress, increased tension, and hyper-irritability. I am unable to walk down the street without being recognised. When asked to Sign-on in Norwich I was constantly heckled by young adults entering the Job Centre and called 'Gary Glitter.' I was chased across the City from the Job Centre by a gang of men who shouted that I was a 'nonce.' One of them was carrying a baseball bat. Any job I had would naturally bring the Company I worked for into serious disrepute. I would consider OPEN UNIVERSITY training. Private Enterprise might also be an option. I am quite interested in becoming a Pyrotechnologist but I have been told that I will be arrested if any fireworks are ever found in the back of my car. If there is any change in the law I would like to open a shop to sell fire-arms and assorted weaponry. It looks like the only solution. I have recently been suffering from a flu virus and have been under the Doctor, but not in a sexual way.

## *Dear Head,*

I was told by Dorothy that I hadn't got to write to you again, and that I should speak to her or Louise in future even though she can hardly be bothered to get up off her fat lazy ass.

1.

Generally speaking we lead a quiet life here. Most of the Residents are fine. It is just the odd one or two who seem to take great delight in telling tales and getting people into trouble. There is a little clique of people who seem to have nothing better to do than pick on everyone else. I know that some Residents here are afraid to go in the lounge when they are there and have preferred to sit on the chairs in the Reception area rather than be bullied by them. The staff here seem to have a very difficult job dealing with them and often seem to take their side.

2.

Last week I went into the lounge to have a game of darts. I hadn't been in for months. When I asked to use the dartboard one of the ladies said:

"And you can piss off! Go on. Piss off!"

She told me that I wasn't allowed to use the dartboard even though I have in the past and it was my dartboard. She also whispered to one of the other ladies there:

"Don't speak to him!" and other things I won't go into.

This group of people have been like this since I arrived. They are very rude and ignorant to other Residents too. When I went to sit in the lounge with my partner a bit later the same people wouldn't even look at us.

3.

I have been in a close loving relationship with one of the other Residents for over a year. We have been very supportive to each other. She lost her husband after thirty-one years of happy marriage about two years ago. Apart from setting the smoke alarm off and having trouble with the front door sticking (which was reported by one of these people as a noise disturbance) we have been friendly and considerate neighbours and get along well with everyone.  The gang have refused to meet with us and tell us why they have so much prejudice and bad feeling towards us.

4.

My friend was refused a pet on the grounds that it would give her neighbours a chance to make further complaints about her but when I repeated what she said the Manager denied saying it. We have both received a letter from Mr Yahman to say that we are continuing to cause a nuisance and that our tenancy is in jeopardy.

He also called the police in.   This is obviously very worrying for us. My friend Christine keeps asking me: "why are they treating us like this when we haven't done anything wrong?"

# Bunderchook

PS In my opinion this is getting to the stage where we need to get a Solicitor involved as it is verging on serious harassment, victimization, and bullying. These are not the sort of people to leave us alone and I think they will go on doing this until someone stops them or refuses to take them seriously. I am worried that sensitive information has reached these people from members of staff and that is why they are so awful to us. I heard one of these people say that "two men are coming round to see you tomorrow!"

Quite frankly, this seems to be mainly about 'labels.'

PPS After the faction here fell out the coffee mornings had to be cancelled. I know they were looking for someone to start them up again. When I asked some of the nice ladies here what they thought about me doing it they were overjoyed. I include a leaflet and petition in support of our offer, but how long will it be until these people are making trouble again and spoiling things?

## Boring old farts

By <u>Godfrey Winklebacker</u> | Published: November 30, 2015 | <u>Edit</u>

Why the same faces each and every week on comedy panels?

# Walking in front of cars

Peter Prezulis was the sort of lad everyone avoided. Even the Canon
on his daily invasions into our classroom refused to look him in the eye.
Peter was the small pale boy who sat at the back near to the grotto.
Fatso never usually went near him. If he did, it was to wind him up, or poke
fun at him. Fatso knew just how far to push him. After an initial
outburst Peter would back down, as Fatso knew he would. For years I
didn't think he could speak any English. He was no good at games
either. He couldn't even hold the rounder's bat without dropping it,
and he ran like an old man awkwardly round the playground. So,
what made me approach him. What made me try to get to know him
better. Was it simply that we shared the same birthday?
I suppose I felt a bit sorry for him. I didn't like to see him bullied or
treated like a second class citizen. My parents were breaking up. We
had to leave in a hurry. It felt as if he was the only boy in class like me.
I wanted to protect him. We were both eleven.
That September we went to the new school.
They called it 'The Holy Family,' but I couldn't see anything holy about it.
I walked up with him one morning.
It was a fine autumn day and we kicked the golden leaves beneath our toes.
We called in "Cliffy" to see the animal cages.
There were flowers arranged in patterns on the grass:
                    CLIFFE CASTLE 1967
We dived in the huge oak-leaf mounds which the park keepers
had heaped together and coughed full of dust. To my everlasting
astonishment Peter swung his foot over every tulip head along the
flowerbed. Then we sloped around the museum. The first room
contained a flashback to the last century. We climbed under the

ropes and went to sit in all the chairs when the attendant wasn't looking. That's where we met up with 'Spellis.' We never called each other by our first names. I suppose we were just used to hearing our surnames being called out every morning on the school Register. We climbed up the steps for a glass of coke at the new cafe and then went through the archway into the arboretum. It was full of strange smells and perfumes. The splash of water echoed down the aisle way. After the peacock cages we turned on our heels and marched through the doorway which led to the car park. We crossed the car park and began our final ascent up Spring Gardens Lane.

Near the top of the hill opposite our new school we stopped to look both ways. A car was approaching from our right. I stood waiting on the edge of the pavement as I'd been taught to do. As the driver approached Prezulis walked boldly out, straight into the path of the on-coming car. The driver screeched loudly to a halt and shouted angrily from his window. Prezulis laughed and then he chuckled. Spellis sniggered too. I gaped in disbelief. I think his face was even paler than usual. I walked quietly across. My heart fluttered like a kite. We scurried in through the gates, breathing a huge sigh of relief that Peter had not ended up like a hedgehog.

Peter gave me the impression that his only ambition in life was to break every puny law he could before he went to the pearly gates. We became regular guests of Sister Campion the Headmistress and were soon introduced to the leather strap hung up in her study.
Peter told me that he wanted to become a 'train driver' when he got older. I thought that was a fine ambition to have. I think he would have made a good train driver too, but one inclined to go through red lights.

We attended the Holy Family School for the next two years. It seemed like a lot longer. There were more bullies in our school playground than the average Prime Minister's Question time. I saw Peter have several close escapes. The last time I saw him walk in front of traffic he nearly got run over. The car's bumper jolted against his leg. He had a scar on his shin after that, but I don't think it worried him in the slightest. We tried to talk him out of it. I think he decided not to risk it again, but I can't be absolutely certain.

As we entered "Woollies" Peter made for the stationary. I had never seen anyone so light-fingered in my life. I resolved never to follow his example. He nicked every ruler, rubber and pencil he could cram in his pocket.
▢ A man-on-a-mission.
▢ His dark uniform.
▢ I cut my finger on his pen-knife.

The door arch of our classroom was peppered in a spray of pellets from his paper-shooter. He fired his pen into the back of many an unsuspecting student. He bragged about shooting pigeons on the telephone wire outside his bedroom.

That was what finally made my mind up about him...

Peter had a cupboard full of conkers which he'd soaked in vinegar. He was unbeaten. His 'king' splattered a husk right into Deegan's left eye and nearly blinded him.

We hunted for "Cheggies!" to see if we could get the other one as well.

He had a collection of keys and hairpins with which he could pick any lock. I saw him take things out and put things back on many occasions. I don't think he was removing things for profit. It was just a hobby. It was a way of proving his prowess.

He was the first schoolboy in Keighley able to make a home-made bomb. His first attempt blew a hole in the road just outside the Mosque. I thought he looked happy when he came in the next day: a blend of delight and utter amazement. A self satisfied sigh. Mission accomplished.

Peter Prezulis seemed to take a pride in breaking the law. He saw it as his birthright. He considered it a privilege. He thought it was funny. All those bible thumping sessions fell upon deaf ears. Their attempts to brainwash him into submission only seemed to provoke him further. He was predestined for a life of crime and that's all we can really say about him.

It was a crisp and sunny morning when I called at the old terraced house close to the park. The lane was littered with milk crates and effervescent crisp packets (his favourite was smokey bacon).

Peter answered the door. The house was paltry quiet. We had to take 'Peter' his dog out for a walk before we set off to school. 'Peter' was a frisky black Labrador which wee'd itself whenever Prezulis raised his voice. This happened to be at ever single lamppost that we passed where Peter-the-dog stopped to plant a plentiful spray of urine.

We walked back from school along the park and cut across the football field close to the great Oak. Near the bottom of "Cliffy" stood an old decaying fountain. I finally plucked up courage.

"What happened to your father Peter. Don't you have a dad then?"

I think he'd died. I don't know what happened to him. I only knew he wasn't there. A vicious rumour circulated. Diarrhoea Spivak murmured something behind her catechism.

Peter Prezulis changed colour several times in the space of a few seconds, his final metamorphosis ending in a sort of greeny blue. I thought it could pour down. He swore at me and stormed away from the park. I watched in horror. His voice shook with emotion. He near snapped my head off. I said I was sorry but I was a bit wary of him after that. The last thing I meant to do was upset him. Peter didn't speak to me again for several days but we did eventually become friends again. He smiled, and blushed ever so slightly. We walked from school, down through the park again.

We stopped below the Horsechestnut trees with our lumps of wood. The 'cheggies' were out of reach even on each other's backs. For twenty minutes we aimed our shots, bringing down a few of the hairy conker shells. We cracked them open with a stone, or simply stood on them. Lifting them up we peeled the jacket away to reveal a lovely shiny seed with a white crown. The reddish brown skin shone in the sunlight. I told him I was sorry about his father. Once again his face turned a funny colour. He began to storm away again but turned back and dropped his head. He smiled. A pale smile with nothing in it. I never thought he would ever cry.

The History exam began. He had come top of the class the previous summer. Peter slid his notes slowly into his hand and read the dates he had neatly printed. Mrs McNulty grabbed him by the lapel and dragged him to the front of the class. He was reprimanded in front of the whole class and his miniature 'bibles' taken to the Headmistress.

Peter lent me a bike and we freewheeled down the hill together. The summer breeze filled our hair. I darted after him. He certainly knew how to ride a pushbike. At the corner we turned into the main road and then on to the cinema. We rounded the corner again and called in the "chippies." We flew down Lawkholme lane and into a small terraced street, bouncing over the cobbles. I glanced in the glazed window where you could just see the outline of his sister getting changed into her uniform. We sat down to eat the best fish and chips in Yorkshire. Arthur Brown's 'Fire' spat its lyrics over the wireless. His mother was invisible. She hardly said a word.

Maybe she couldn't understand English.
I don't remember her.

At the Christmas play Peter Spellis sat in the row ahead. Hymns were being sung. We could see a nativity scene up on the stage. Throughout the performance Prezulis soldiered away at his duffle coat. By the end of the evening he had cut off most of its toggles and loosened a few more. Spellis told me he kept a line of milk bottles on his windowsill filled with fluid. I thought it was disgusting. I couldn't understand where it came from. I didn't see the point.

I left to go to the Grammar School a year later. Spellis came with me, but we were never close again. By then Peter had gone his separate way, whatever that was. We no longer built dens in the bushes or knocked-off school to toss huge lumps of concrete at diesel trains.

We dropped Spellis after he became too lippy and invited Tony Howley to join our pack. He came from a single parent family and was very highly strung. If you lifted a hand he would blink, so much that everyone in class called him 'the Blinker.' I remember his obsession with Jane Fonda, whose sexy pictures in Barbarella outside the Ritz became the focal point of many trips down to the street corner.
Prezulis liked 'Lulu' best. I thought that a very bad choice as she resembled my neurotic raving mad mother.

I got a job with Tesco's to earn a bit of extra pocket money in the evening some years later. It was their first store, on the edge of the bus station. I was just seventeen. Stephen Hibbert came with me. He's in the Australian Navy now. His father owned the local brewery and a fleet of racing cars. I was surprised to see Peter Prezulis working there. An ideal location when you think.
Peter blushed and kept on blushing.
"Gals," he smiled. I think I embarrassed him. He just wanted to be left alone.
I noticed how Peter always worked in a particular spot stacking shelves. I walked over to join him. He pointed to a gap in the tins where you could look right up the check-out assistant's skirt...

What really made my day was the night Hibbert was searched leaving the building. I never saw anyone turn such a bright crimson. He tried his best to hide the 'Wagon Wheels' at the bottom of his satchel but was still dragged off to the Manager's office and reprimanded.
Peter Prezulis winked at me.

I waited at the exit for the boy who was going to bash my brains in.

He'd been tormenting me for weeks for being a virgin.
"Howard's gonna get you!" I walked out of the back door to meet my nemesis. After a couple of minutes the Supervisor dragged me off him. Peter laughed when I told him.

The last I heard of Peter Prezulis was in the Keighley News. He'd stolen a motor car and crashed it into a wall. After that he'd tailed it. The police called at his home. He denied everything at first. One of the Officers drew attention to his wrist watch, which had its glass cover missing. They took the missing watch cover from a bag, and hey presto, it fit exactly. That's when they brought him in for questioning. Maybe his luck ran out? I'll never know, because I've never seen or heard of him since. Wherever he is, I wish him well. God's love. God's speed. Peter. Peter Prezulis.

## Tell the truth and shame the devil

By Godfrey Winklebacker | Published: March 21, 2015 | Edit

Supposing there is a devil to shame of course.

## Lying is great

By Godfrey Winklebacker | Published: March 21, 2015 | Edit

To have the courage to lie and be proud of it. That is the essence of human kind. To out-manoevre your opponent. To subterfuge, to mislead and to profit. And if you are caught out to laugh about it. Some of the best liars in the world have been acclaimed by their supporters as *Saints* and *Prophets*.

Comments

## The Cock

My shift was cancelled for the whole week and I was called into the Manager's office at the back of Cambridge Station. A few hushed whispers as I passed the Secretary at her desk.

It was a dark room with a board of stern faced critics sat at a long wooden table.

I sat twiddling my fingers and no doubt looking extremely awkward.

"We received a report from the Officer at Kings Cross concerning your arrest. Until we reach a sensible conclusion to the matter you will be removed immediately from your job."

"You will be transferred to the **Carriage and Wagon** depot with a stipulation that you do not come into contact with any females!"

# Carnage of the flowers

We crept out through the gate,
one by one,
tucked in close to the wall,
with hands at prayer.
Down the garden lane,
to the flower beds,
brute-back Deegan,
snarling in the distance.

Worming all over the grass,
tossing Peter's satchel in the oak leaves,
keeping a sharp look-out,
and breaking into a sprint,
we,
massacred all along the empty benches.

Prezulis the thief,
got to the buggers first,
intercepting them right down the middle,
then Spellis got stuck in,
flying in with both legs on the diagonal,
trashing a whole avenue of blooms,
seven, eight, nine in one leap.

He yelped,
lashing out with his foot kicking,
scything through the air,
losing his footwear.

Stray dogs slavering,
thundering through the park,
the snap of stalks,
sniggering like girls,
we chopped the lot,
beheading as we went,
showering the flower-beds with petals.

# Greed is good

By Godfrey Winklebacker | Published: March 21, 2015 | Edit

Don't let anyone mislead you or call you "Scrooge." It's great to have lots of dosh. To sit in your cellar at night counting all your loot. To ride in your carriage raising your glove to the adoring multitudes. Never having to worry about paying the bills. To send your children to *Public* Schools. To pretend that money is the source of all evil and that war has never gained you any land.
As Frank Sinatra once said:
 "I've been rich and I've been poor. Believe me: rich is best!"

## Touching for the king's evil

By Peter Smith | Published: March 21, 2015 | Edit
In medieval times the King was believed to have divine powers.
How else could he have been king, without the power of the lord?
Simple peasants only had to touch his collar or the rim of his boot to be cured of things like scrofula, head lice, cholera, and dysentery.
Another thing the King strongly believed in was *shagging his step-son*.

Comments

## Groping carries mandatory life-sentence

By Rumplestiltskin | Published: March 21, 2015 | Edit

Unless you are royalty of course.

# comments

# Workman gets 22 years in jail

By Godfrey Winklebacker | Published: March 21, 2015 | Edit

The workman arrested by the terrorist squad was given twenty two years in custody the other day. It seems rather severe, but what is the point in being a 'Judge' if you can't throw your weight around once in a while?  He was picked up on the street carrying his 'work-bag.' In it were found a flag of the Queen, a trowel, a hack-saw and some nails. Okay, he had intimated he might want to take a trophy home to his wife but I'm a bit concerned that one day we might end up jailing people for *'thought-crime.'*

Comments

## L A W S

By Sarin | Published: March 19, 2015 | Edit

Just an attempt by the Establishment to impose order and restrictions on the world.

## Comments

# Orcs

By [Rumplestiltskin](#) | Published: March 18, 2015 | [Edit](#)

# Mehmet says

By [Sarin](#) | Published: April 8, 2015 | [Edit](#)

Mehmet says he can evict anyone he likes. He says that he doesn't have to *prove* anything; he only has to *believe* it to be true!

Mehmet says that he has to take *every* complaint seriously. That includes complaints coming from liars with an axe to grind who just happen to be his closest friends.

[Comments](#)

# Bunderchook hailed as giant sea crab

Robert scowled at me across the floor.

"You're wanted in the Office.  Mr. Stanley.  You better be quick, you old *Groper*."

(It was just after the **milk throwing incident** and the arrest of Neil Clitcher for murder).

Mr. Stanley was smiling for a change.  He offered me a seat.

I'd been expecting this for five years.

"When you first applied for your job you didn't tell us you had been in prison…"

(Flashing my knob, Your Honour).  *By the way, your son is an absolute cunt.*

"We have no alternative but to suspend you because the complaint came from a <u>member of the public.</u>  One of your neighbours has just written to the Trust Director to say that you're a convicted *rapist*."

## More labelling and intimidation by Wherry Housing

By Peter Smith | Published: April 7, 2015 | Edit

Dear County Court,

I have been served with a Court injunction by Wherry Housing Association. The hearing is for Monday 13th April at 2.30 pm.  I do not wish to attend, as I no longer live at the above property, where I have been harassed since I moved in. This was because I was sent to prison a long time ago for contacting my ex partner on the telephone (it was not malicious or threatening). The police went round telling everyone about me. Confidential information was leaked by the Housing Association to my neighbours in an effort to stereo-type me.

A lot of what has been said in the witness statements is totally untrue and has been manufactured by a clique of people at the scheme who have completely refused to speak to either me or my partner for whatever reason.

I do in fact get along with a lot of the Residents and have been running a coffee and social morning for them for the last two years. I also run a Creative writing group on the site.

I have been in a close loving relationship with a lady close by, who lost her husband four years ago, for the last two and a half years. We have never done any of the things the gang have accused us of. In fact, it is us who have been the subject of abusive threats and obscene swearing in the middle of the day and night. All the complaints against me are alleged to have taken place when I was at my partner's address, but none are about where I actually live myself.

The effect of all this on me and my partner has been extremely damaging. We have thought more than once of getting a Solicitor but they can be very costly. I had to have a brain scan due to head pains recently and I had to call the Emergency ambulance a few days ago due to sickness. I am out of work at the moment due to prejudice. I'm finding it very hard to start again due to people's bias. I would find it very difficult to pay such a huge amount of costs and would humbly ask you for a bit of help and understanding instead of punishment.

## Angry red-faced priest

By Rumplestiltskin | Published: April 5, 2015 | Edit

We called in the Slipper Chapel at Walsingham the other day. An old fat priest was arranging the altar cloth when we walked in. I told him I used to work there fourteen years ago and asked him if he remembered the former Director, which he did. He told me that when the last Director died *the Marians* had to give up the shrine because there was no-one left to take it on. He said that the last Marian had been ordained over thirty-five years ago.

I told him that Pope John Paul had been a Marian.

"No he wasn't!" snorted the priest.

"Yes he bluddy well was!" I said. "I have a letter at home from him saying so."

## Labels labels labels

By Godfrey Winklebacker | Published: April 4, 2015 | Edit

Don't you get sick of being labelled as one thing or another? This kind of obsessional pigeon-holing emanates from a severe shortage of brain cells and a desire to over-simplify an individual's more complex character.

Comprende?

## **Marilyn**

What's the first thing I did when your friend 'Andy' died (he used to help you with your shopping)?

I offered to do anything you needed help with.

**I'm sorry if the note caused you any distress. I always thought we got along. I simply wanted people in the home to know the truth and that I had not done the things some people have said.**

**Don't you think it's important that people should know the truth?**

I did not have sex in the Reading room. I had been doing some sit-ups on the floor when you glanced in as you passed and there was no-one else in there with me. I heard you had been off your food for a week.

Why on earth did you call the police? What was so serious about it? I just don't understand why you did that (so, it was Didwell's idea you call the police?).

I didn't think you liked the Didwell. Now you are calling her your friend?

# There's one thing about Jesus

By Godfrey Winklebacker | Published: April 4, 2015 | Edit

The Middle East of two thousand years ago was just as violent and turbulent as it is today. Still the same greedy politicians clamouring for power and factions of one sort or another fighting for dominance.

Whether you believe he was the Son of God or not, Jesus spoke out against the Ruling Government, which during that period happened to be Roman, and as we all know, anyone who is seen as a threat, or who has the audacity to stand up to Authority will be punished severely by all the methods available.

# Hitting sixty

By <u>Adumla</u> | Published: April 3, 2015 | <u>Edit</u>

I don't like it and I won't have it.

## Durst confession definitely unsafe

By <u>Godfrey Winklebacker</u> | Published: April 3, 2015 | <u>Edit</u>

A poor disturbed businessman is found in a semi-comatose state with a gun and some drugs in his jacket and no-one smells a rat!
If the fuzz didn't plant it I'll eat my hat.
They wouldn't even turn up to give evidence.

## Farage says: "Political elite not to be trusted!"

By <u>Godfrey Winklebacker</u> | Published: April 3, 2015 | <u>Edit</u>

Do we really need to be told?

## PACK ANIMAL

By <u>Rumplestiltskin</u> | Published: April 2, 2015 | <u>Edit</u>

Self sacrifice
Equality for all
Respect for cretins

Baa!

# Freedom to fight in holy wars

By Peter Smith | Published: April 2, 2015 | Edit

# Sex Offender's Register

By Rumplestiltskin | Published: April 1, 2015 | Edit

There has been a Sex Offender's Register in the UK and different parts of the world for about twelve years:

This is how it may affect your life:

o unable to travel without prior agreement

o forbidden to stay in a house with anyone under eighteen years of age

o prevented from seeing your own children

o subject to frequent police visits, searches, and interrogation

o subject to permanent monitoring, assessment, and screening

o stopped from finding regular worthwhile employment

o unable to find suitable housing or get car insurance

o shunned by small badgers and *Conservatives*

o friends relatives and associates also tainted

o regular searches of your bank account, phone, and e-mail

o required to register every year at a specific location only

o friends and neighbours informed

o labelled and ostracised for the rest of your life

o your passport seized and your card marked

o acclaimed as a warped and twisted individual by all do-gooders

o questioned by the Authorities wherever you are

o prospective partner's informed

o forced to divulge intimate details about your love life

o your property seized and your assets frozen

o your guilt proven and your card marked with very little evidence

o stared at by pea-brains and small mongeese

*    vulnerable to arrest at any time of day or night

*Every so often you will be bullied into having your fingerprints and mug-shot re-done.*
*\* Failure to notify a change of address for instance could result in five years imprisonment.*

**LESS THAN 1% OF REGISTERED OFFENDERS ARE WOMEN.**

The Sex offender's register was originally for serious sex offences only. Dozy Magistrates and curmudgeonly Judges will always side with the Authorities. These are some of the circumstances for which you could be placed on the catch-all Register:

+ looking up a skirt
+ placing an ad in a Lonely Heart's Club column
+ sitting on a park bench
+ wolf-whistling
+ showing your arse on a building site
+ using a pair of binoculars
+ chatting up a member of the opposite sex
+ slapping the Secretary's backside
+ touching a virgin
+ sending a text message
+ giving someone a photograph
+ looking through a window
+ brushing against a passenger on a train
+ smiling at anyone good looking
+ wearing a Gannex raincoat
+ making a sexually *inappropriate* remark
+ wearing a see-through bathing costume
+ phoning an ex partner
+ giving a lift to a stranger
+ taking knickers from a clothes' line
+ parking outside a school
+ reading pornographic literature
+ taking a picture of your girlfriend
+ portraying violence in a painting
+ looking across the street
+ getting into an argument
+ foul or abusive language
+ statutory rape and homicide
♦ taking your dog for a walk

More police powers!
A REALLY BIG TWAT IS WATCHING YOU.

# Into bondage

By <u>Rumplestiltskin</u> | Published: April 6, 2015 | <u>Edit</u>

As I understand it there are various forms of 'bondage.'

These are:

- tying with rope, handcuffs, or net stockings
- whipping
- ball and chain
- bandaging
- gagging
- drinking the piss (also known as 'taking the piss')
- the wearing of tight footwear, blindfolding etc.

Those who indulge in this kind of behaviour have my sympathy, but I really think something must be wrong upstairs. Special uniforms are optional.

**<u>BUNDERCHOOK TOO PROVOCATIVE FOR WEB SAY WELSH SHEEP-FARMERS</u>**

By <u>Adumla</u> | Published: April 5, 2015 | <u>Edit</u>

Snoop dogs from the *single brain cell* spy centre down the road have been flooding the Home Secretary with calls:

"You need to see what he's writing. He's a wrong 'un Mrs!"

"You need to take him off before he corrupts the very fabric of society."

Thankfully, the Good Doctor, has faithfully stuck to his task without any breaks in communication so far (a brief but ultimately unsuccessful attempt to take him off the air almost succeeded a year ago).

Complaints have been as regular as clockwork from GCHQ about the content of the site and its predisposal towards: homosexuals, Muslims, and furry green leprechauns.

We are facing CLOTHES DOWN folks!

# W a t e r

It is six months since I gained my PhD in Toxicology. I specialised in the field of rat-poison and was able to concoct a totally new virus in my final year: it consisted of a finely-balanced solution of weed killer, depleted molecules of uranium, a ginger-nut slice and a variety of neurotoxins.

I carry it wherever I go in a small rucksack with a skull and crossbones logo on the front.

I am pressing on with my research into a new carcinogen based on a hybrid compound of arsenic and strontium. I have yet to perfect my latest bacillus which had me itching all over my face when it first appeared in the test-tube. The drains are looking a bit off-colour, but I have more important matters to worry about.

On my duty days I take myself off to the nearest bus-station. It isn't long before we are coasting along near a suitable canal or river complex. I glance down at my bag. The infection is safely contained in a sardine can.

Everywhere I see water. Everywhere I see the dry desert slaked by the thirst of a nation. I rise from my prayer-mat and bless my holy oracle.

Deliriously I bound up the hill and race along the escarpment. My sandals are bursting with sand as I run down the wall head. I'm dancing with joy.

My main holder has a red rust round its lip. I clamber over the entrails of a pipe-cylinder spreading my anthrax seeds.

Everywhere the melon shaped truths.

The lake calls out for my deliverance, the sun toiled beams lapping against the water's edge.

Feverishly I grasp at the lid. I'm hysterical and covered in a kind of phosphorescent afterglow. I turn and raise my arms up to the sky. The sound of my rapture echoes all over the valley. I'm splitting my sides. I'm euphoric with a sense of mission.

*I see water: everywhere I see water.*

I walk calmly round the mouth of the weir to where an angler is just about to cast his rod. The white upturned bodies of trout float like random particles on the surface, and I know, I'm convinced, beyond any shadow of doubt, that my work is still in progress.

# Father why do you bleed

Where the land and the sea,
Meet in harmony,
And the oceans and fleece touch the sand,
Where the yellow sun shines,
And the heavens-in-rhyme,
Father,
Why do you bleed?
Where the hills greet the sky,
You return the dark fields,
The furlough, the plough and the stars,
In the hedgerow you roll,
Your face in the stream,
Father,
Why do you bleed?
Where you bathe the bright seed,
In the west where you ride,
Sunning the air which we need,
Too strong for my eyes,
You light up the earth,
Father,
Why do you bleed?
On the heels of your soul,
Cross the skies where you fall,
The storm wind, the clouds, and the spring,
In the sunset you weep,
Reclined at your feet,
Father,
Why do you bleed?

# Small birds sing

I can't say,
that small birds sing,
or that you are weird or anything.
When I listen to their sound,
it makes me smile,
it makes me want to grow feathers.
If you had been,
my one and only love,
all that I heard when the sun awoke,
If you had been there since,
the dawn of time,
my angel and my sparrow.

# What little bastard

What a little bastard,
he is,
what's that little bastard there,
doing
in my house...
y little bastard,
y little sissy git,
get out now,
get outta the door,
before I take me strap off t' yuss.

What's this little bastard doing here,
making a sound when he eats,
Where did he come from...
Just standing there,
What's this little bastard doing in my house?
Whose little bastard is he anyway?

Stop crying or I'll hit you!

# Know your enemy

By <u>Usuli Twelves</u> | Published: March 17, 2015 | <u>Edit</u>

1. Seek to understand your enemy's thoughts

2. Take them into your confidence: identify their weaknesses and goals

3. Find a way to *use* your strengths against their greater numbers and try to catch them off guard

4. Only meet your enemy on solid ground

5. Divide your enemy

6. Make your enemy fearful

7. Never attack your enemy without a safe line of retreat

8. Cut your losses and if need be gain the time to fight again another day

9. Spread false rumour and disinformation about your enemy

$Accuse your enemy of being a 'radical'

# Moralists

By <u>Godfrey Winklebacker</u> | Published: March 22, 2015 | <u>Edit</u>

People who think they know what's true and want you to believe it as well.

# The death of Christianity

By <u>Godfrey Winklebacker</u> | Published: March 22, 2015 | <u>Edit</u>

I think it's fair to say that Christianity is on the wane and wouldn't last five minutes in the company of a devout Muslim.

# Good king Richard

By <u>Rumplestiltskin</u> | Published: March 22, 2015 | <u>Edit</u>

The once demonized bad-boy of British history is to have a Christian burial at last having been murdered many centuries ago by thieves greedy for his empire. According to history Richard III was the rightful and legitimate king. By all accounts he fought bravely to the end in spite of his physical ailments. When he was dead or dying one of the future king's soldiers shoved a sword up his bum. Somewhat typical of victors I feel. Our bravest king, however, died at Hastings…

# Cliff Richard

By <u>Rumplestiltskin</u> | Published: March 22, 2015 | <u>Edit</u>

My friend Bob worked in the music industry. He said that Christians up and down the country were even more judgemental than the ordinary man in the street.
He told me that girls in the nineteen sixties were always throwing themselves at pop stars. He said that they were only spilling the beans now because of the huge financial incentives offered by the police.
I told him that the Authorities were only interested in having a good laugh and couldn't care less how much anyone suffered.

Comments

# Simon knows everything

By <u>Rumplestiltskin</u> | Published: March 22, 2015 | <u>Edit</u>

Chris said to me the other day that: "Simon knows everything."
(He's the leader up at the church by the way).
She couldn't find her black knickers.
I suggested she ask Simon.

### Britain's most wanted man

By Rumplestiltskin | Published: March 22, 2015 | Edit

Britain's most wanted man was captured by police and put in jail after going to live in Spain and trying to make some kind of life for himself. He had not committed any crime. He had simply not told the Authorities where he was living, probably in the hope that he would not be harassed and labelled for the rest of his life.

Comments

## No need for cameras

By Peter Smith | Published: March 21, 2015 | Edit

The Specialist Circle law enforcement officers at HMP Bure Valley House have informed us that we do not need any surveillance cameras around the building. They would cost a lot of money and would need to be permanently monitored (along with all the Residents).

I can only assume that we have them here already.

Comments

## PRIVATE AND CONFIDENTIAL

Your Honour,

Could you please read what I have written about the surrounding circumstances:

This is not the life I would have chosen for myself, but I sincerely believe that I am a decent caring person given the chance. It is with deep regret I find myself here today. All I want is a quiet space to relax in and enjoy the best relationship I have ever had. I openly admit to making some very silly mistakes in the past. Close to eight years ago I contacted an ex-partner when I had been told not to. It was not an attempt to get back with her, and neither was it at all malicious or threatening, yet I have suffered continual harassment ever since. Before I went to live at the Zoo the police went round telling everyone there that I was a dangerous Sex-offender, which is simply not true. They applied for a special order and as a result of telling the Magistrates I would attack my ex-partner they were able to put me on a Register even though I had not committed any other crime. This became common knowledge to my neighbours because the police were always calling round and asking questions about me. It made it very difficult for me to settle down or have a normal fulfilling life even though I did make some friends there and worked hard to make a new life for myself.

I left Bure Valley S.ithouse voluntarily in April because I was always being picked on. It was only a particular group of neighbours (one of whom's son is a serving police officer) that were always reporting me, but I was not the only one who was bullied by them. When we complained to the Housing Association about *their* foul language, noise and physical threats nothing was ever done about it. In fact, the Housing Association Managers seemed to be on very familiar terms with them. They have accused me and my partner of all sorts of things we have not done. These people completely refused to go to mediation or to speak with us even though an outside Mediator had been arranged.

Before I arrived my partner Christine, who had just lost her husband to cancer, was being reported on a regular basis for such things as boiler noise, and feeding the birds in her garden.

Thankfully, I do not live at Bure Valley Zoo any more, and I was not living there when the Housing Association handed me the first Injunction papers. They seem intent on ruining my relationship and labelling me for no justifiable cause. Just a few months ago the new Support Manager (Card-carrying Bryant) warned my partner that if she continued to see me she would end up losing her bungalow. I believe it would be against my human rights to prevent me from visiting my friend, as long as I behaved considerately and did not cause any genuine grievance. I do have other friends there too.

I really don't know what more we can do to get along if these people completely refuse to talk to us or even reveal why they are so against us. As I said to my partner only a few days ago, there is nothing to prevent them reporting us again just to get us into further trouble.

# A senior police officer

By Peter Smith | Published: March 21, 2015 | Edit

A senior police officer said today that parents needed to take more responsibility for their offspring. He was very much in favour of more surveillance to prevent them 'falling into bad company' and before they could be 'radicalised' by evil and malign influences on the Internet.

"We live in a very dangerous and unpredictable world!" You can say that again. The Pleb urged parents to be more *vigilant* and to find new ways to spy on their teenage sons and daughters *before* they were forced to raid anyone's home and seize their computers.

The police chief said they were doing all they could to prevent people from being taken in by "extremist ideologies."

This could include shutting down certain social networking sites.

**Regrettable, but essential for your protection!**

*Dear Mr Simpson,*

I am still having problems using the Internet because of State interference.

I have two issues to bring to your attention:

1 Phone companies like Vodaphone are being allowed to take money off people (on their mobile phones, after the phone has been topped up) even when the phone hasn't been used. I had £10 in credit, but the phone company took it off at the end of the month because I hadn't used it. This is being done to other people besides me and we have found it almost impossible to get it back without spending a lot of money we don't have.

Before I moved into my current property the police went round telling people all sorts of distorted rubbish about me. Why is your Government letting these idiots get away with this? It makes it impossible to settle down, get a job, or become a *normal* member of society. Don't you realise what is going on, or do you simply not care?

Sheeps Manor,
Anyoldstreetcorner,

16, Grabcunt Lane,
Elizabethan London.
4 September 2012

## Dear Mr Simpson,

I was sent to prison three and a half years ago: for contacting my ex girlfriend, with whom I had lived for a short period and who still had some of my property in her house.
I did not touch anyone, or threaten anyone. I was not charged with any sexual offence or offence of violence. In the *undisputed call* I actually tried to apologise and reassure her. There was also one disputed text message. I admitted sending a text message, but we couldn't agree which one, so I had to go to what was called a 'Newton Enquiry' at quite considerable expense. Shortly before the end of my sentence (I was recalled for going on a library computer) the police applied for a SOPO order because they wouldn't have had any more excuses to keep harassing me or of justifying their employment.
As a bi-product of getting the SOPO and the lies told by them in Court they were also able to put me on the Sex Offender's Register for life too.

I am constantly being harassed by them and can't get on with my life.  Once again they turned up on my doorstep this weekend arguing with me in front of the neighbours, demanding to know if I had developed any new relationships, and demanding access to my home.  I do not stand any chance of having normal friends after they have been round spreading their rubbish about me.  I have already told you about a certain Associaton refusing to let me live in any of their property after they have been to talk to them.

I asked what the police wanted to talk to me about and if they thought I had done anything wrong.  They said they didn't know if I had done anything wrong.  I said I hadn't so I asked them to leave me alone.  I asked them to leave several times before they went and was careful not to swear.  They told me that they can make 'unannounced visits' whenever they want to and that if I do not let them have access to my living accommodation they will get a warrant and smash down the door.  Apparently I do not have *to talk to them*, but the legislation says I have to let them inside.  What kind of country are we living in?
I have written to the Prime Minister about my position and about the thirty-odd complaints I have made against the police.  I did make a mistake with the date on my letter unfortunately.  The IPCC eventually *upheld all my complaints* after the Norfolk force stated that it was nothing to do with them.

What I would like to know Mr Simpson.  If the police do return and continue to bully and terrorize me, what do you intend to do about it, if anything?
Incidentally, my mother saw you crossing the street last week and you said "hello."  Do you know her?  She says you have lost some weight.
She took your appearance in the town as an omen of an imminent election.  I don't know what put that thought in her head.

## Dear Keith Simpson,

Thankyou for your letter dated 5th July about Broadland Council's position and their appalling attitude.

Just to correct a few *minor* points:

1 I did *not* lose my place at John Boag Dog-kennel due to anything I did.  I had already been served with an eviction notice due to the reasons I stated before.
I did try to visit my sister in Ireland, but since the police put a SOPO order on me near the end of my sentence, and as a consequence were able to put me on the Sex Offender's Register, my life would have been ruined there too.  What infuriating rubbish.
In fact one of the police officers from Norwich said that if I hadn't come back they would have spent the next year searching for me in order to bring me back from there.
*Now at last do you see what vicious scum the pigs really are?
When is someone going to stand up to these people?
I don't know where the council are getting their information from but you can see from their letter that they are joining in with the labelling process of the police.

2 I have asked the police and Probation several times why I am under MAPPA (Multi Agency Poke Prod and Asshole) when I have not committed a serious sexual offence or an offence of violence. All I get is: "the PPU are a law unto themselves!"

I presume you read my complaints to the **police complaints commission.** I have forwarded a copy to the *Minister of Justice.* If you can help please do so. They won't.

3 Nothing at all in the letter from the council about their reasons for refusing me a property they had previously offered me; on account of my background. What does 'I can't comment on Mr ~Bunderchook's background' in this instance actually mean?

4 The way the hostel scheme is run makes it very difficult to get any normal housing. What they do is keep you in the hostel for a year or so, and then move you to another hostel for even longer, so you never actually get out of the system or get shut of them! At least I am away from having to sign every few hours and constant summons to the police station for a 'friendly chat...'

5 The letter states that I was adequately housed in 2008. Will someone please go round and give these people a good kicking. What utter rubbish...a lower needs band, because I am in a Probation hostel along with rapists and drug-addicts? They have got to be kidding.

6 I was taken off the housing list for no apparent reason this year and had to re-apply so it is not true that I have been constantly on the list.

7 Why are these wretches still having meetings on me and still being allowed to interfere in my life?? You can't get rid of them. I would like to know which government conferred this 'received authority' onto people like them or is that too much to ask?

# Good day Mr Simpson.

I believe you are still our local M.P.

I wonder what you thought about the excellent way David Davis defended Andrew Mitchell in the recent smear campaign by the grand British bobby? Pity there's no-one to defend the ordinary citizen from their lies and persecution...Sorry you can't get involved. Wouldn't want to damage your reputation.

# Dear Tone-deaf Simpson,

I am writing to complain about my home being invaded by the police again today. It happened while I was running a coffee morning for older people here.

How much longer is your Government going to allow these bullies to get away with it?

How much longer do you think it will be until you have another mass riot on your hands? Could you please tell Mr. Cameron that the Blueberry riots weren't about people from deprived backgrounds, but about genuine hatred of the police (unless he had time to read *the full report).*

Once again, we have your Government trying to impose even more surveillance (Chris Grayling) upon people who have already suffered the brutality of life and all its paradoxes.

I don't know what Theresa May is doing in her job if she can't control or understand the police and their tactics. I am including a copy of my index offence, which I have sent you once before. Knowing what liars these people are, I wouldn't put anything past them.

And no! I can't afford a Solicitor, as you have been told a thousand times before.

# Dear Himmler,

I wonder if you or a member of your party would like to comment on the recent not-guilty verdict in the case of Coronation Street star Bill Roache and the huge cost to the tax-payer? I'm sure if he had been a poor ordinary member of the public he would have been sent to prison for a large number of years in spite of his age. I, as you may remember, was sent to prison for two and a half years, over five years ago (and I am still getting harassed by the fk... idiots now) for contacting my ex partner on the telephone (one non-threatening land line call and one disputed text message)>Now *at last* do you and your Government understand why people riot in the streets?

*Sincerely.*
*Bill of Rights.*

# Incarceration Works

Prison has become a revolving door with the population rising year by year and the cost growing out of all proportion to the improvement of society. Even recent attempts by the Minister for Justice to supervise more people in the community has met with stiff opposition. Although the cost of imprisoning increasing numbers of people cannot be sustained there are many people in society who think that prison is the only answer and that the only reasonable way of punishing anyone who steps out of line is to lock them firmly behind bars whatever the cost. In a very competitive and pressurized world an influx of new laws has increased the number of law-breakers. Prison recalls are booming: shouting in the street, an argument with your partner, late for an appointment, we don't like your attitude, you wore shorts in our interview – back inside! Dragged along in handcuffs by a hovering mob of flatfoots. Many offences would have been viewed as trivial in the past. Imagine trying to explain to a soldier in the trenches that you could get two years for sending a text message or that you would have your life completely ruined by telling someone you still cared about them.

The Prime Minister said recently that the claims brought by prisoners due to the blunders made by prison staff amounted to many millions of pounds. Cases of salmonella and medical negligence abound. A lot of prisoners are detainees or foreign nationals. Prison has become a dumping ground for every social delinquent, misfit and reprobate. Members of society who are most enthusiastic about incarceration include the police and the Probation service. We have known for years that the police are willing to sell information to the highest bidder (but don't tell anyone I told you…). *One sided and distorted gossip* is spread across the daily news and internet. Long-winded and expensive reports written by 'experts' follow offenders wherever they go no matter how *biased, false or inaccurate.*

Some commentators believe that a lot of people don't really need to be cooped up in prison and that they are not really doing anything worthwhile or productive there. They think that prison actually makes people worse and that due to the intolerant and prejudiced attitude of people who are too quick to judge others they leave prison with a mountain to climb and the increased likelihood of further offending. Society has created an underclass-of-citizens incapable of finding work or any kind of happy fulfilling existence. Many members of society couldn't care less how people decline through the process or how many men go steadily downhill with every dismal step leading back to the jail house. Time to reflect on one's actions is seriously diminished by the level of care, the disturbing nature of prison life, and the unbalanced turmoil besieging one's mind. How can a place which is so full of violence, drug abuse and harm be a centre for nurturing someone back into normality? Politeness and tolerance are in very short supply. Honesty and reality a thing of the past.

A small number of individuals are completely incapable of improving. There are a group of prisoners so dangerous and anti-social that prison is the only answer. These people can never be rehabilitated or adjusted back. Their life is so damaged and disrupted that having them out in society would only lessen the safety of others and would capitulate to a deterioration of standards for us all.

There are plans to make prison even tougher and to keep people there for longer if their behaviour justifies it. This doesn't take into account the attitude of prison staff who are always ready to give a prisoner a bad report or to pigeon-hole them into obscurity. How would an ordinary member of society feel if they were given a *behaviour warning* for hanging their coat up at the end of their bed, for wearing a pair of boots out in the yard, or for asking a sensible question when you are being bullied by a loud-mouthed and aggressive tyrant with an IQ lower than an old world primate?

*Power produces resistance to power.*

You obtain 'enhanced status' if you are willing to jump through hoops.

Meaningless tasks such as 'penny-washing' are handed out like gold dust.

Inmates are deliberately matched with someone who is their violent opposite.

(I was once attacked in the middle of the night by a prisoner who was suffering from Schizophrenia. It was a terrifying experience. I reported it to one of the Officers the next day).

"So how do you know he's suffering from schizophrenia. Are you a fucking expert?"

Well actually I worked with people just like him in the health service...

"Not really," I said. "He told me so himself."


Many Officers come from a military background or the deli counter at Tesco's. There's a personal officer scheme which was being touted around recently. It was an attempt by the Establishment to turn prison officers into social-workers...A man had hit me from behind with a piece of broken pottery because he said I owed him a mars bar. I consulted my Personal officer for a response...

"Who's your *Personal officer?*" she asked me, chewing her gum and examining her nail-varnish.

"You are, and you have been for the last six months," I said.


Sharing with another male in such a small claustrophobic space can produce a lot of friction. There is often no privacy. It can be degrading and miserable, but no-where near as bad as the journey to court in handcuffs on the prison bus, which must be the most depressing place on earth. Your file lies open on the desk ready for the escorts to read all about your personal background and charges.

A smirk on their face.

I've met with every kind of villain you can think of. Men who could read and men who couldn't. Men who had raped their daughters and priests who insisted they had done nothing wrong to the choir-boys.

Each individual left prison even worse than when they entered. Not a single person was improved by the experience and many went out alone with the same demons and obsessions as before.

Not a single programme of treatment halted their beliefs or radically changed their thinking. Many risk-levels actually increased to the delight of those running the show.

I've seen men jump head first from the balcony in an effort to end it all. Men suffer complete breakdowns when their loving and faithful wives write in to say they are seeing a police officer.

Young men who could have been developing deep and meaningful relationships slit their arms open with desperation after months of goading from the Screws.

Yes, of course it works to keep people locked up for long periods of their life.

It certainly helps the politicians: when there's an election looming.

# Comments

# Phone of the new life-savers

"Hello Samaritans, is anybody there...?"
 A moment's silence.
Could it be yet another sex-caller?
I glanced at my colleague and yawned.
Today's *Day-leader* turned from her file and took a sip of her wine.
 "How are you *feeling* this morning?" I asked.
 I could hear heavy breathing.
 "I've just lost my wife," a voice answered.  I could hear sobbing.
"The house has burnt down, and I was fired from my job."
"Our only daughter was killed yesterday crossing the road."
 He gave his name as Chad.

"Well, things could be a lot worse," I said.
"I've just been diagnosed with lung cancer," he whispered.

"Have you ever thought about taking your own life?"  I said.  "Seriously."
"It could be the best thing for you.  I hear they have run out of *argon gas for* the present but there is a perfectly good multi-storey car park in the town centre."


# Rat, Buffalo, or Squid

We strapped him into the hoist.

*Glasses on.*

We lifted him from his bed: he sailed through the swing doors and into the bathroom with a gleeful and cock-sure howl.

His lordship was lowered into the bath.

*Glasses off.*

The hoist was pulled from under him as the water flowed from the tap.

*Glasses on.*

His mother smiled.

*Glasses off.*  Wiped.  Sprayed with condensed milk powder.

His hair was shampooed. He winced. His eyes watered.

A towel was carefully dabbed in the corner.

*Glasses back on.*

After two hours of soaking and splashing like a bull elephant he was shipped back to bed.

The glasses were cleaned several times and passed back and forth.

His pants were at half-mast. As his bed-pan was pushed under his bottom he wriggled petulantly.

He shrieked like a young pterodactyl. Adam smiled and nodded over the rail. *The wondrous bed-pan.*

We worshipped it like the lord of Hosts!

Pam rushed through the swing doors to see what he had done.

For two rancorous weeks he'd been unable to produce a single dump and the bellyacher was beginning to wake the whole bloody neighbourhood. He wouldn't sit out in the garden. He sulked if the TV control wasn't placed in its correct position on the pavilion. He even refused to have a peep at 'Men-in-boots' on-line.

*I was ready to use a cricket bat to reduce the swelling.*

What have we here? We both looked at each other.

His mother made the sign with her hands. He stared across the room poker-faced.

She made the sign for 'Buffalo.'

Adam yelped and went into an orgasmic frenzy.

I stood behind her and raised my hands closer together.

He started. He jolted. His eyelash flickered.

I made the sign for 'shrew' and went to pack my bags.

Then all hell broke loose.

# Object of fertility

Do you remember,
Dear Eva, when I kissed you and played 'Red roses?'
I was so tired then, and old beyond my years.
Thoughts of dear death now rend the thunder clouds,
and snare me from this ignominious void,
Our wedding band the lightening of the guns.

The red hot liquid, which once erupted,
from my fiery breath, now mocks me in the dungeon,
with our jouring fate.
A fleeting second crushed the transient star.

I tossed and turned amid the midnight lamp,
and for a moment wandered blind among the gas,
the final flash, seeming but a prayer away.

The once proud idol of the fatherland,
whose pact on ashen faces greets the generals gone,
sweet Lucifer christened the artist's tongue.

We shed the mantle of earth's peace,
but how were we able to drink up the seas?
Two iron crosses I do bequeath…

History, tear up the tattered verdict of this court,
I lay on you my fondest sons of youth,
in memory of the supersleuth: *Wolfbain*.

And now, my dear Eva,
lend me your arm,
the three of us: my mother, you and I,
we'll sleep forever,
in this chambered grave.

# The rebellious king

I lay untroubled ages deep,
to rise again, from death from sleep...
from brittle nature flaked with white,
heartbeats renew the pumping blood.

The fetching Moon in paper wings,
which pierced my side as if by lance,
the awning weeps with honeyed lips,
this glistening fruit of winter's tears.

All ladyland an open womb,
whose bright earth blinds my amber
eyes...
violent violet and the purple flowers,
trace thrum across my battle scars.

The arching sapling spreads its green,
the burning Sun bestows my crown,
I soar above the harvest ground,
like spelt beside the plain.

The beating of the bardic hymns,
no longer sound where silence sings,
she sleeps beneath forever chaste,
the rustling armour of the leaves.

Where on the wind my kinsfolk lost...
the spectral army of the seeds,
our languages and laws are host,
to vagabonds, in Avalon....

Let shades surround my pastel peace,
sad nature cut my vocal chords,
I shudder at the thought of cold,
between two triangles of Time.

# Ephemera

I see your smile begin within,
the fresh first flower of holy spring,
as you come gliding through glades to meet,
closer to me, like the whispering leaves.

And then I saw your blushes bloom,
the burgeon glows with summer warmth,
like tender blossoms here to hold,
upon the midnight apple grove.

As we caress in twilight song,
our kisses spent our seconds gone,
when emerald leaves fall Autumn gold,
the dusky mellow Moon beyond.

Shall I recall in later years,
sweet tones,
when you were just a girl,
the winter Phoenix purges cold,
goodbye my love the love is old.

Your smile it breaks unchanged by days,
in love again, a moment's tears,
the curling mouth the passing Sun,
vernal bluebell sweet daffodil.

# Acushla

Sometimes,
when the west wind sings,
and softness distracts my eyes,
from this world of mocking-birds,
in fingers from the stage.
Sometimes from a darkened pool,
the sunlight caressed my dreams,
I could but soothe the day's retreat,
four shades of latched blue...
Sometimes when the morning breaks,
each tender love I give you,
I feel the draught beneath my feet,
running to meet your smile…

# TO YOU MY DAUGHTER AS YET UNBORN

To you the essence of my dreams I give the Sun the Moon and Stars...
I give the incandescent fuse of Jupiter and Mars.
I give the mountains lofty peaks,
a sullen chase of nimbus clouds,
a trail of nuzzling gossamer,
black kestrels over plain.
I give the hills perspiring pearl: wild swans that wing from Coole,
an aspiration through the mist,
the yellow lamp of dawn.
I give the flock whose journey south,
is fraught with rose and thorn,
the tiles of every rooftop,
the flicker of the tide.
I give a thousand beating hearts,
each universe of sand,
to you my daughter, as yet unborn,
a sea of pink flamingoes.
I give these scattered pictures of,
the world and all its blend,
each sennet in the tree-top,
every petal on the stream.
Each branch upon the juniper,
every tooth of cinnamon,
every seed upon the stalk,
each crystal from the vault.
And if your cheek were ever raw,
from hail or tiny thing,
I'd bring each tender bird that sings,
a rainbow at your door.

## BUNDERCHOOK
### personal Asbo for:
# Sir Bernard Hogan-Howe

**dob:** *Unwilling to comment*

*You will abide by the following conditions until your retirement on a stinking rich pension:*

1 Abide by the conditions of your personal Asbo.
2 Not misquote yourself unless under extreme pressure.
3 Provide the most unflattering photo of yourself whenever you are in the news.
4 Not conduct a relationship with any vulnerable person or miner.
5 Not grope, fondle or expose yourself when out on operational duties.
6 You will investigate the allegation that the Met is an institutionalized and bigoted band of storytellers.

*Failure to abide by these conditions will result in severe embezzlement and the compulsory seizure of your bravery medallion.*

## Bunderchook
### Anti-Social behaviour order for:
### Baron Prescott
### dob  May 31 1938

For the foreseeable future you are requested to abide by the following conditions:

1 You are to refrain from having your chauffeur drive you to the property of one 'Michael Heseltine.'
2 You are to remain indoors after 17.30 hrs on weekdays.
3 You may not pinch the bottoms of any female MP's or members of the European Parliament.
4 You are to refrain from drinking on board ship.
5 You will remain ignorant of Grammar Schools.
6 You will continue to speak in a lumpen-proletariat accent stumbling over the occasional long word.
7 You will take lessons in the noble art of gentlemen.
8 You will avoid punch ups in the street or any other act which may cause offence to the B.N.P.

*Failure to comply with these conditions may result in serious loss of liberty or further decreases in your intelligence!*

## BUNDERCHOOK
### Anti-Social Behaviour Order for:
### General  Leopoldo Fortunato Galtieri Castelli
### dob  July 15 1926

*The following conditions must be implemented WITHOUT FURTHER DELAY:*

*1 You will refrain from electrocuting Jorge Rafael Videla or Roberto Eduardo Viola.*

*2 You will be punctual and keep your colour clean and your buttons gleaming.*

*3 You will not assassinate any member of the Government without consultation with Battalion 601.*

*4 Before kidnapping any member of the public you will liaise with the 11th Baronet of the Burns.*

*5 You will only meet behind closed doors.*

*6 You will be made a scapegoat.*

*Failure to bribe  your enemies may result in serious loss of prestige.*

## BUNDERCHOOK
### Anti-Social Behaviour Order for:
### Charles Saatchi
dob  *June 9 1943*

Until further notice you are subject to the following conditions:

1 You will reside in permanent opulence and prosperity.
2 You will refrain from kerb cruising red light areas or from handling a white powder.
3 You will only use your credit card for essential items.
4 You will not visit Italy.
5 You will avoid dining out in any restaurant within a fifty mile radius of Glasgow.
6 You will reward any petulant or vindictive behaviour with another sweetener or tv contract.

Failure to comply with these conditions could result in **strangulation** or a long term of **imprisonment.**

# Online ASBO

**PUT A STOP TO BULLYING AND INTIMIDATION**

**<u>Personal Asbo's</u>**

Have your own unique personalised ASBO written and crafted by the expert:

Prevent you from terrorizing the neighbourhood

Keep you off the street

safe and reassured

no situation excluded

guaranteed approval

**Specially reduced rates for:**

*Members of the Clergy, PPU and Armed Forces*

*Senior Citizens    Chief Constables*

*Serbs, Arabs and Croats, Streetwalkers and Tarmacers*

# Russians support Assad to exterminate 'Extremists'

By <u>Usuli Twelves</u> | Published: October 10, 2015 | <u>Edit</u>

## Comments

# Big hairy monster!

By Usuli Twelves | Published: September 23, 2014 | Edit

During the nineteen-seventies DLT was a regular host of 'Top-of-the-Pops' on British television. I found his whole manner irritating and disagreeable. I will never know why no-one knocked his annoying block off; although they do say it carries a minimum twelve month jail term, and of course fighting is wrong (ask any branch of limp wristed *Evangelicals*).

After being found not guilty on over twenty charges of assault the British Justice system thought it appropriate to have a re-trial on the one remaining charge in which they couldn't reach a guilty verdict (the police were able to root up yet another charge in the meantime). This was to prove that no-matter how rich and famous you were, you would still be treated 'just like everybody else.' DLT has now been found guilty on the one remaining charge by a majority of 10-2. As he said in his own words: "this whole business has ruined my health. I hope it will be over by the time I'm eighty."

Members of the Prosecution were seen shaking hands and blessing the ground on their hands and knees. Happy as a pig in muck, as the saying goes.

Well, Dave. You may think it is *finally over*, but the authorities will never let you go now, and there are not that many more disc jockeys around to make a scapegoat of. .. One guilty verdict is as good as thirty. You will be branded a pervert for the rest of your life and be subject to regular visits by the flat-foots. Your home could be raided at dawn from now till the end of your days with your name added to the Register. And what did you do which was so disgusting. What terrible deed did you commit which has cost the country millions of pounds in wages? You brushed against a woman's breasts as she was walking down a corridor in 1995. Shame on you! There isn't any punishment I can think of which will heal the horrendous harm you have done. Having said all this, your pompous and irritating manner is as nothing compared to the figure chosen to decide your fate. "All options remain open!" I can see you now, standing in the dock with your finger held up high as your punishment is revealed, and a few extra months added to your sentence.

 * The real monsters of course are the long list of cretins who brought this case to court in the first place and who hoped to profit from the destruction of another person's life.

# Cameron's heart is mended

By <u>Surloin Steak</u> | Published: September 19, 2014 | <u>Edit</u>

My heart really went out to David Cameron as he sprinted anxiously northwards. (I thought Gordon Brown looked a lot happier. He still gives me the creeps though!)

Cameron: "It would have broke my heart if Scotland had broken up the United Kingdom!"

What 'United Kingdom' is this Mr Cameron?

One whose frontiers are constantly being invaded and whose laws are written in Brussels. One where freedom of speech is slowly being eroded and where multi-culturalism has destroyed any sense of British spirit and identity.

Where there are street riots against an unpopular and invasive police force and where cameras monitor our every movement.

Of course, if Scotland *had* voted for independence that would have meant less power to Westminster and a severe drop in the number of citizens it was able to boss around.

## Boy with brain

By <u>Usuli Twelves</u> | Published: August 29, 2014 | <u>Edit</u>

A massive police hunt started today for a young boy taken from hospital by his parents.

British police are determined to find him. Their family car is being tracked across France in a bid to bring him back.

A police spokesman said that they were extremely concerned: "We need to know where they're going!"

He finally admitted that "although no crime has been committed YET…" they would leave no stone unturned until he was found.

The Head of the Thames Valley force had to wipe away a tear when he told the waiting conference room about the lack of number plate recognition cameras in another part of the world.

# Low ranking Judges would be lords of porn

By <u>Sarin</u> | Published: March 17, 2015 | <u>Edit</u>

Three would be Judges were sacked today for allegedly looking at naked men and women. It makes a change from looking at children. An older more experienced toff wanted to let them know who was boss. After viewing the material the Lord Chancellor said it was "totally inappropriate for a Judge to be looking at indecent images. This sort of behaviour is completely inexcusable."

One of the poor Judges had been suffering from "depression," but this was not accepted as a plausible reason for him to masturbate at work. You'd think they would know that everything they did was being monitored. Perhaps they wanted to be caught?

(I used to think you could get away with anything if you were a member of the OLD BOY'S NETWORK)...

## More pus from the Jubilee Family Centre

The church elders were rubbing their hands in glee today at the prospect of five hundred new homes being built on the edge of town. 'I want this hall to have two hundred regular churchgoers by the end of summer. We will soon need to build a brand new hall to accommodate everyone. God is with us my friends. Let's see how many more suckers we can lure through the door?'

# Mullah accused of wearing beard

By <u>Sarin</u> | Published: March 17, 2015 | <u>Edit</u>

It's getting a bit much when you can't even sell alcohol to underage teenagers.   How are you supposed to know how old they are anyway?  This is the same as cigarettes, but not the same as writing **inflammatory literature.**

# Game of thrones

By <u>Sarin</u> | Published: March 14, 2015 | <u>Edit</u>

I often imagine David Cameron or another toff sitting happily on their throne dreaming up another rule to add to the statute book, but there are some people I would never like to think about.  Some of the tyrants from the past for instance: Idi Amin, Mary….house, Pol Pot, Edward I, or Glenys Kinnock.  It's a place where you can really get your head round a problem, where you can read your favourite novel, or play with your Spirograph.  Some of my best ideas have come to me in the thunderbox. I bet it won't be long before spy cameras are forcibly erected in everyone's private throneroom though.

## Bure Valley Sanatorium

By <u>Rumplestiltskin</u> | Published: March 12, 2015 | <u>Edit</u>

Spoke to Sonia over at the Rest home today.  She was taking part in the bingo. Sonia has drooping tits and a four o'clock shadow.    She's 27 stone, but used to be a marathon runner.  For the last eight years she's been doing an OU course in Psychology and Social Sciences.  Sonia said she was once six feet tall.   I guess she must have shrunk somewhat.  The best bit was when she said she was related to *Queen Elizabeth I.* "So were you married to Prince Charles as well?"  I asked.

## comments

Sheffield Hillsborough

## Blurred lines

By Rumplestiltskin | Published: March 11, 2015 | Edit

I saw Marvin Gaye's relatives 'crying' outside the court today as they were awarded millions of pounds in 'damages.' What a load of rubbish the jury system is.
They didn't even bother to listen to the *original* track.

Comments

# Clarkson gets into gear

By Rumplestiltskin | Published: March 11, 2015 | Edit

Ok, so your head nearly touches the roof and you're a loud mouth prick sometimes, but who in their right minds wouldn't give two front teeth for a swipe at a BBC Exec?
I like Jeremy Clarkson for his wild eccentric views.  He's outspoken.  That's a good thing!

## Prat shett

By Godfrey Winklebacker | Published: March 13, 2015 | Edit I met Terry Pratchet in the nineteen sixties when I was growing up. He didn't seem very extraordinary and was wearing biking leathers.  I thought he was a bit difficult to get on with at times but very courageous in the way he took on the Establishment over the right to die with dignity.

### ISIS mercenaries hounded by British Police State By Sarin | Published: March 15, 2015 | Edit

What a brave and courageous act.   To follow your faith.  To give up all that you own.  To leave the people you love. To join fellow martyrs in healthy sacrifice.   If I was a Muslim living in this thought shackled and oppressive post-colonial country I would be going up the wall.   British armies spreading their gospel around the globe were never stopped at the border and asked for a 'pass-port.' Having been thwarted once the British police must be licking their lips. Turkish authorities have arrested would be fighters at their behest.

*Why is it so frigging hard to get out of this country but so easy to get in?*

# Mafia boss praised for ordering deaths

By Sarin | Published: March 15, 2015 | Edit

When Trevor McDonut interviewed a famous mafia war-lord he questioned him about his credentials.

"You had the power of life and death?"

"You ordered the deaths of….."

In an attempt to make him feel *'guilty'*.

Doesn't every Government and Politician around the globe do exactly the same thing.

# Offensive weapon

By Adumla | Published: March 16, 2015 | Edit

This extremely offensive object has been the subject of many a long discussion. Without it there would be no human life. It has been responsible for more crimes than anything else. It is so evil it has to be covered up and tucked away.

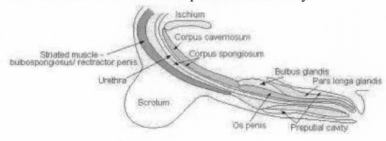

Comments

# Not interested

By Peter Smith | Published: March 17, 2015 | Edit

Why anyone should be remotely interested in what big fat Cyril Smith did forty years ago is completely beyond me.

# Match Commander guilty of mass murder

By Peter Smith | Published: March 17, 2015 | Edit

Today Commander David Duckenfield admitted he lied a quarter of a century ago at Hillsborough football stadium:

• The buck stopped with him.

• He directly caused the death of 96 innocent people.

• He shifted the blame.

• *All truth is simple. Is that not a compound lie.*

**A worthy and scaffold-hungry Scapegoat?**

# Too sick to work

By Rumplestiltskin | Published: March 18, 2015 | Edit

Brian phoned in sick today. His friend's dad had died and it brought back painful memories.

# Mum's the word

By Rumplestiltskin | Published: March 23, 2015 | Edit

I hate asking for favours, but sometimes you just have to swallow your pride. I recently asked my mum for a small loan.

"Look mum. This is very kind of you, but I don't want to leave you short."

"You won't be leaving me short," she said.

"Yes, I will. You are only five foot."

(She still thinks Charles should be king).

### Richard the 'Lion-heart'

By Peter Smith | Published: March 23, 2015 | Edit

Following one of his most famous victories Richard the 'Lion-heart' encouraged his soldiers to hunt for jewellery and precious stones out in the desert. The only problem with this was that the Crusaders perceived the treasure to be hidden among the small intestines and bowels of the thousand or so Muslim women and children they had captured, who now cowered beneath their blades.

We are always being asked to condemn Muslim extremists for their barbarism and cruelty. Pictures appear daily on our news depicting them as *less-than-human*.

The West has always seen itself as a paragon of virtue and the chief arbiter in cases of morality.

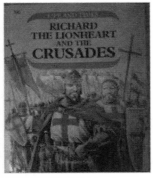

# Mehmet Yahman
# Mehmet Yahman
# Mehmet Yahman

By [Bird Dung](#) | Published: September 11, 2015

**Bunderchook** arrived home today with a Reception Committee waiting for him in the street. Former neighbours at the Bure Valley leper colony had been making still more complaints.  A daily log had been kept of his activities:

- Banging a door shut   Glancing at a neighbour's kitchen wall     Letting down tyres      Scratching cars Having sex
   Using the laundry   Laughing     Leaving a pubic hair on the lavatory seat     setting fire to Harry

- Sending a note to a former Resident explaining the difference between truth and total bullshit

- Having a letter delivered to the wrong address: upsetting the Occupant

*Mr Low told *yet another story*. He swore he saw a shadow cross the corridor and that someone had knocked on his window late at night. His mother was not at all happy.

## Bv Bird Dung | Published: September 11. 2015

## EMERGING FROM THE DRUM OF DEATH'S SHADOW

Alabaster,

bone,

the tat of old tail-feathers.

Clothed in a red life-jacket,

birding.

My fire-devil,

like a sprung out steeplejack,

glad of the sky-chalk,

becoming whirlwind.

# RIDING A CHARIOT ACROSS THE BAY OF NAPLES

It is not with lark's wings,

Or the smash of chisels,

That I carve my way,

Through a heart of steel,

On a route of blue flame,

But with a chariot,

Drawn out,

Across the bay of Naples.

A steaming froth of silver,

Nostrils flared,

Over the spray I dash,

Lighting up the continent.


## Not so funny now

You laughed,

You hooted,

You sniggered.

Along with your friends.

On the sofa,

Where we had shared our good  times.

The way you did in the evenings...

You had us all in hysterics.

Sloshing away on the blower.

Peering into the night,

Your cardigan splitting,

Your strap loose and overfed,

Your pants at half-mast,

Pissing yourself.

# WINGED BIBLE OF THE ASTRONAUTS

From the book of knowledge,

we found our store,

godless creatures of the sky,

like eagle-owls with wings of gold.

Swooning in the temple of our stars,

the cross-bearing,

witch-finding angels.

Roped in our nets:

Moons like marsh gas,

the Reaper's coat of many colours,

spitting like gnats,

To the promised Land's,

desk pool of miracles,

across the sands,

on our bird reborn.

New orders in the light of night,

the fire-winged serpent,

red giant glowed,

above Lazarus.

Stained in our seat,

old shepherd,

kindred spirit of the walking clouds,

sharing our passage and our souls.

# ALFRED LORD TENNYSON WITH LOTS OF SALT AND VINEGAR

From the chippies we sprinted,

Down Lawkholme lane at eight,

the citizens of our fair town,

drunk as lords....

Me and Chris,

Skully and Meg,

Tubby and Phil.

Burning our hands.

Hoisted quickly aloft,

I clung to the top,

Where the horn and the steam,

Like a Big Daddy,

Thundered on either side.

"Blinkered!"

We sighed

And prayed to heaven.

# ROMMEL'S BROWNING REVOLVER?

A gun was found today,

Under the floorboards.

I have an inkling it flew in from Chicago,

Marked 'automobile parts'...

Dum-dum bullets...

Firing pin?

Museum de Belgique...

Stamped with a swastika.

What I had it for is anyone's guess.

# BAFFLING PROOF OF THE SANITARY TOWEL

Mysterious puzzling lees,

Sodden and intimate curls,

In the bleak and cracked dark,

Of the closet.

Revealing,

Your secret movements,

Before the Exodus.


In the heat of the moment.

Last rain of the summer.

Drowning in sorrows,

Discovered long after.

Mingled with what-might-have-been,

Scarlet and blocking the road,

nameless.

We covered you over,

the corner of ruins.

# Theft of parcel

By Godfrey Winklebacker | Published: September 14, 2015 | Edit

Dear Sir or Madam,

I wish to report the theft of a small parcel containing computer software which was stolen by the Support Manager working for Wherry Zoo on Friday 11th September.  Not only has this organisation been supporting bullying and intimidation on the site it has now confiscated an item which it knew belonged to me.

I asked my partner to pick up the parcel for me. It had been wrongly delivered because I only realized at the last minute that e-bay still had my old address.

The Support Manager completely refused to hand over the package and kept it for herself.

I would greatly appreciate your help in the recovery of this parcel as soon as possible. I know this organisation to be extremely evasive and dishonest.

# .Stewart witch-hazel

By Sarin | Published: March 24, 2015 | Edit

Stewart gave me a strong piece of wood today. He said it came from the old oak forests of Ireland. He makes catapults at £30 each but I'm not sure if they would be powerful enough for my intentions.

## HOWEVER BIG YOU GROW

However big you grow,

little flower,

just sitting there on the doorstep.

However big you grow,

no matter what your mother says...

Whatever place you go,

in the sunrise or the sunset.

## Power

By <u>Peter Smith</u> | Published: April 9, 2015 | <u>Edit</u>

What could be better than to see the rich and famous in trouble. Mankind is a selfish and power hungry animal.

## COMMENTS

# What to do if you are caught out lying

By <u>Peter Smith</u> | Published: April 12, 2015 | <u>Edit</u>

1. pretend it never happened

2. blame it on someone else

3. tell another lie

4. accuse someone else of lying

5. stand on your head

6. laugh your blumming head off

7. make a vow never to get caught again

8. run and hide

9. join an organised religion

• Get your accuser arrested for *exposure*.

*Any offers?*

# Ark of the Pagan

We carried them in, after the long drought,

the books which Solomon had given.

And dried in the Sun, for twenty years,

until the heron came, clutching a single spray,

swallowed up the fog lamps:

*A pole-cat of priests,*

*the suitcase of Elvis,*

*A crowmarsh of woodpeckers,*

*birched at the backward river.*

*A six-headed rhino,*

*lama's eggs,*

*in the black mirrors,*

*coated in mistletoe;*

*Aristotle, Hercules,*

*My clown's make-up.*

*A plunder of Vikings,*

*the comb of Rameses,*

*woad of a Highlander's torch,*

*a gander of goblins,*

*drip-white-coal,*

*distilled with the torque of persistent regret.*

*A bootnail of Horace,*

*13 round clothes-pegs,*

*My auntie's seduction,*

*the palace of the two winds,*

*runes written in semen,*

*a lamb's brain,*

*and one candlestick of nuns,*

*hovering near the confessionals.*

# News of the World

By Adumla | Published: April 18, 2015 | Edit

What did the Sun journalists have which the News of the World journalists didn't have?
Political clout. That's all.  Oh, and a different jury. From now on journalists will not have to go to prison, but prison officers and plebs will be given fifty lashes.

# Illegally parked

By Adumla | Published: April 18, 2015 | Edit

I went to register my move yesterday at the cop shop.  He took another photograph of me with my glasses on and told me to be careful if anyone came in.

I said I wasn't bothered if anyone came in.  I wasn't afraid of them knowing why I was there.

An old lady in front of me rushed to the desk:

"I've reported a car on the road six times already this year for having no tax disc and it's still there!"

"I think it may even have a bald tyre."

Get a life someone

They don't have to have a disc displayed any more you OLD AGE PENSIONER.

# Migrants

By Sarin | Published: April 19, 2015 | Edit

**I see the hungry and oppressed faces staring towards me from the keel of the ship.  The bow bobs on the water.   A burst of sunlight as their eyes peer jubilantly towards the shoreline. Reaching for my birth control button I wait for the hatch to open...**

## The difference between Catholic priests and black magicians

By Peter Smith | Published: April 12, 2015 | Edit

The main difference between Catholic priests and black magicians is that black magicians don't promise to punish you even after death if you don't believe in their hocus-pocus.

THE VERY REV. FATHER RAPHAEL.

# God

By <u>Adumla</u> | Published: April 18, 2015 | <u>Edit</u>

What kind of God would punish you for your time spent here on earth?  Surely that God would be as vindictive, merciless and cruel as any Judge?  Not to fight your enemies. Not to oppose the despot.  To turn the other cheek.  What kind of crackpot would do that?

# Revenge porn

By <u>Adumla</u> | Published: April 18, 2015 | <u>Edit</u>

So.  We are not even allowed to post photographs of our conquests on line now.  Shame on you!  It is something of an assumption to call it 'revenge.'  I think it is more likely 'justice!'

(Yet another attack on men).

## Gossip never happens

By <u>Adumla</u> | Published: April 18, 2015 | <u>Edit</u>

The leader of the Jubilee Family Church told me that no-one in his gang spreads any gossip, and that if he heard of anyone doing that he would stop them.   I told him a story the other day about a lady in the Sunday congregation.  She said she had heard that I took off all my clothes and streaked down the corridor.  She said she was sorry to have missed it.  I told her it never happened.  When I told Simon about this he turned round on his bike and sped up the road.  Born again Christians.  Don't y' just love 'em!

Comments

# Don't believe in sin By <u>Adumla</u> | Published: April 18, 2015 | <u>Edit</u>

Sin is something dreamt up by the moralists in our society.  It doesn't exist.  Its total bullshit.

# Man beaten on board train

By <u>Adumla</u> | Published: August 22, 2015 | <u>Edit</u>

Today a young Muslim was pronounced unconscious on board a train where he had been set-upon by a gang of young heroes.  They were described as 'incredibly brave,' and have already been awarded medals of honour for their unspeakable courage in the face of so much diversity. Time people were segregated once again?

# Cops to take mandatory lie detector

By <u>Adumla</u> | Published: August 22, 2015 | <u>Edit</u>

#Well, they are hardly likely to do it voluntarily.

# Another Afro-American execution

By <u>Adumla</u> | Published: April 9, 2015 | <u>Edit</u>

Yet another black male has been cut down by a white American policeman after being stopped for a minor traffic violation. Eight bullets. For what? The police continue to lie and cover up their mistakes. This is just the tip of the ice-berg.
Mind you. The Politicians are just as bad.

# Return of Saladin

By <u>Adumla</u> | Published: April 9, 2015 | <u>Edit</u>

It's been on the cards for a while. The return of the Great General. A wise magnanimous spirit who moulded a strong army of adherents. Able to repel invaders and put down internal strife. Who gave all his riches away to the poor and needy. Who was kind and merciful.

# Farage pariah  By <u>Sarin</u> | Published: April 21, 2015 | <u>Edit</u>

At the end of the debate the rest of the leaders quickly rushed to shake each other's hands and cluck to high heaven. I saw them gathered round each other in the far corner. Farage was left alone to arrange his papers. I didn't see him talking to anyone.

# ISIS freedom fighters detained  By <u>Sarin</u> | Published: April 21, 2015 | <u>Edit</u>  Yet another family were detained and prevented from crossing the border by Turkish authorities working on behalf of the British police force. Their children were all placed into *protective custody*. Why shouldn't they fight for their religion?

# Female of the species
By Usuli Twelves | Published: April 22, 2015 | Edit

Spoke to 'the Boss' the other day.  She was fuming.  Why didn't I let her know mum was crazy.  Teachers!

# Muslim men make the best lovers

By Usuli Twelves | Published: April 22, 2015 | Edit

My sister should know.  Never went near anything else for years.  "Only jealous!"

# Demonic gibberish

By Usuli Twelves | Published: April 22, 2015 | Edit

I've come to the conclusion that so called 'speaking in tongues' is merely demonic gibberish meant to impress the ignorant rabble and goad them into servitude.

# Attack on churches
By Sarin | Published: April 22, 2015 | Edit

I've been attacking churches all my life.  Nothing so mean and corrupt as organised religions.

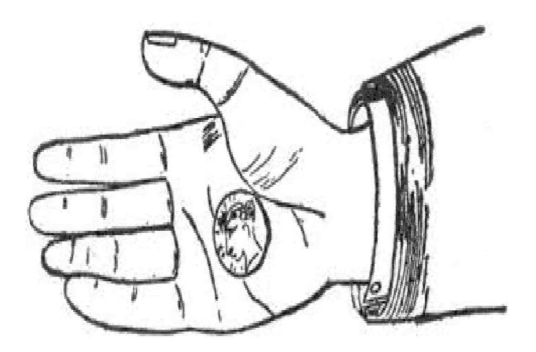

# Deserted Island in the middle of Pacific

24 June 2013

Dear Mr Davis,

I understand that you are a very busy man, but I would still like to tell you my story. I do hope you will find time to read it. I am not looking for sympathy. I just want someone to know the truth.

In 2004 I became very upset after a relationship break-down and thought about taking my own life. I don't usually feel this way but I was very disappointed about how my life had turned out. I was working as a Support worker and teacher of sign-language in Oxford. I was also very fed up about getting old (I was nearly fifty) and I was suffering from long periods of migraine. I just felt as if my life had been a failure.

As I consequence of this I sought help from someone on-line and was able to persuade them to send me an old fire-arm. When it arrived it was in pieces and I was too afraid to touch it. I had never had anything to do with such things before. It was actually a museum piece and was welded in parts, so it was not actually able to work. I just stored it away in pieces under the floorboards. I didn't really know what to do with it.

In 2005 I began living on and off with a local Health Visitor. I found her a bit difficult to be with sometimes but I persevered and thought my feelings might one day grow. I didn't tell her how I had been feeling. She was very loving towards me but I just couldn't respond in the way she wanted. She had two small children who I treated with the utmost care and devotion at all times.

Our relationship came to an end because of my inability to be comfortable with her physically. Our relationship was never quarrelsome or abusive, although I did discover she had been seeing other men from the internet when I couldn't give her the intimacy she deserved. I continued to go back to the house even when our relationship was over. Sometimes she would order me away and then the next minute she would ask me if I would be staying the whole week. She knew that something was wrong, but I just couldn't tell her what it was because I didn't want to disillusion or disappoint her.

Near the end of our relationship when she had started drinking a lot I admitted one offence of non-sexual 'exposure' when a shop assistant who had been serving me on the High Street looked into the changing area and saw that I was partly unclothed. The incident lasted approximately 2-3 seconds. She simply handed over the trousers, turned and walked away. I was arrested two weeks after the incident and dragged in handcuffs through the crowded shopping mall to the Central Police Station where I was held for ten hours, while the person I was supposed to be looking after wondered where I was.

I was never able to explain what had happened to my former partner, who comes from a very good family, although I do know that the police went round to her home, where I still had some of my property, to tell her I was a Sex-offender. She finished with me by text on the same day.  As a consequence of admitting the offence of 'exposure' I was given a three hundred pound fine, ordered to attend a Sex offender's treatment programme every week for two years (at great personal cost and difficulty-it was about fourteen miles away from where I was living and working), and due to a recent amendment to the law placed on the Sex offender's register for five years (if I had been under the age of 35 it would have been for three years! A very important fact). Every week I attended the course I argued with the Treatment managers who thought that any act of exposure was a sexual offence and an extremely serious abuse of women. I told them that the human body was not dirty or indecent and that due to the nature of my job I saw people naked every day, and it never upset me. I also told them that if a woman of a similar age had been seen semi naked in the changing room her life would not have been turned upside down, and she would not have had constant visits from the police or been ordered on a course.

I do a lot of mountain biking and am a former body-builder. I was reprimanded for my attitude and for wearing shorts when I came to the group. They accused me of deliberately showing off and warned me that if I cycled over in shorts again I would be in breach of my Court order, and that they would take me back to Court.

When I told them that among my previous girlfriends had been a Senior Probation Manager and a serving police-woman they accused me of being a 'fantasist.'

I still continued to visit the home of my ex-partner and check on my belongings. My former partner knew I was going there. She told one of our friends about me. She told some of our friends that she'd had me banned from the town (where I was living) and she continued to send me the occasional text message like: 'fuk off u impotent loser!' and 'squishy little white dick.' I tried not to take any notice. She reported me after she had seen me in the supermarket where we had shopped each week together.

In 2007 I sent her father, who was a Professor of Literature, a copy of my most recent book of poetry. When she got her hands on it she handed it over to the police as a form of harassment (most of the work inside wasn't about her, but was work I had been assembling for some years). I thought it would be my final work before I died. Shortly after that her son saw me locking the door from the top of the stairs and told his mum. This is the same little boy I had carried in my arms to bed each night, and read him his bedtime stories.

I was sent to prison for two years for possession of a fire-arm without a licence after the police raided my holiday home (the police kept adding numbers to the total number of rounds found with it from a handful up to thirty).

I received six months custody for sending the poetry book, and
eighteen months for the night her son saw me locking the door.
A painting which I had done for my ex-girlfriend, and which had hung
on the wall above the fish tank for years, was taken down and
destroyed because they found a note on the back saying: 'You gave
me a dream of a happy home. Something I never really had,
and I gave you this little picture which I mistakenly thought would be
my last.'
While in prison I suffered an unprovoked attack from behind by a man
who said I owed him a Mars bar. Against the wishes of the prison staff I
called in the police, who gave the man a 'Caution.' I had been
covered in blood and needed hospital treatment.
Upon my release I was ordered to live in a hostel along with drug
addicts and serious Sex-offenders. This continued for month after
month. On the first day of my release the police turned up and
accused me of new offence.  They said that I fitted the description down to the ground.
I was only released when the video footage in the bookshop confirmed my alibi.
I spotted a file bearing my name which said: Sex offender:
_Dangerous to women and children,_ written on the front.
When I complained they said the only reason they could find for me
having  'dangerous to children' written on my file was the night when
Benji saw me simply locking the front door.
While at the hostel the Residents were invited to do a talk about the
work they had done. It was part of a programme to get us all working
again. I was the only one to speak. I told them about my work as an
Instructor in Occupational therapy, about my work at the 'Samaritans,'
and about my duties as a British Rail Signalman. I was accused of
making all the other Residents feel inadequate by the staff. One young
man offered to talk about his job, but the staff said that 'drug's dealer'
didn't really qualify.


When I returned to Norfolk to be near my mum, a retired
Schoolteacher (and step-father, who was suffering from bone cancer,
but who has sadly just passed away) I was prevented from going to church
by the police who had been contacting every single person I knew or who
 had been on my e-mail or phone because they said I was a
Dangerous Sex-offender. I was told that I had to sign every hour at the
desk in the new hostel even if I was ill, or be recalled immediately to
prison.  I was given a warning after walking a girlfriend (a local
Businesswoman) to her car one evening after we had been to a music
concert because I was a few minutes late for my signing. Three
warnings and you were back in prison to the delight of the Probation
staff. The staff wanted to know her name and where she lived so that
they could send the police round and tell her all about me.
I continued to ask the police and Probation why I was a MAPA level 3
when I had not been charged with either a violent, or a sexual offence.

Just before Christmas 2008 I was late back from a healing group I had

been attending at Norwich Spiritualist church and the Probation staff

were going to get me recalled back to prison in the morning. I went on

the run, and eventually ended up living in a caravan a few miles away

from where I had been living in Oxfordshire. I was free to visit my doctor

and dentist. I was close to friends I had been prevented from seeing. I

was able to visit my old work colleague Roger Wicksteed, who nearly

died after a serious stroke. I was able to visit him and thank him for all

his kindness and friendship during my time inside. I returned back to my

girlfriend's house one night to see what had happened to her. Some of

my property was still at the house but some of it had disappeared.

I meant her no harm. I certainly didn't intend to frighten her or any of

her family.

*She was openly masturbating at her computer in front of*

*her two young children to strangers on the internet.*

*I was very shocked and saddened by what I saw.*

Her son Benji saw me in the garden. Against my

better judgement I rang her an hour later. A policeman answered and

put on a funny voice. I wasn't sure if it was her or not, but I told them I

was very sorry about what had happened, and that I never meant to

hurt her. I hadn't had the opportunity to explain what the fire-arm

business was all about without the police going over there to tell her I

was going to kill her. I wanted to clear the air of a grave misunderstanding.

Two days later I was arrested coming back from the bike-shop in

Banbury. Even though I did not resist arrest in any way I was dragged

from my car and beaten at the side of the road by two burly young

officers and returned to prison. I tried to make a complaint about my

injuries at the time but the prison staff were very obstructive and I had

enough to deal with. I felt very tired and under stress.

I tried to represent myself in Court over the breaking of my restraining

order. I was charged with breaking it by phone contact: one undisputed

landline call, and one disputed text-message-I argued that anyone could

have sent it. There were no Witnesses to the text message. Nothing I did

was either malicious or threatening.

I received one and a half years in custody for the phone contact and another

year for not notifying the police of a change of address because I was on the

Sex offender's register due to the 'exposure' years before.

I had to serve the full two and a half years in prison.

The policeman who had been visiting my ex girlfriend, and who had

bragged about spending time with her on more than thirty occasions

sat there grinning at me when I received my sentence. I had asked

him in cross examination; "What have you done to discourage the

idea that I would ever harm my ex-girlfriend. You know that it's

absolute rubbish!" He refused to answer.

I was told that the good references I had managed to gather would

not be admissible because I had not presented them in time.

Added to the two and a half year sentence was the time I had been on-the-run. There seemed to be no end to the nightmare. My friends in Oxford, most of whom were members of the academic community there (some were my old employers), were appalled at the severity of my sentence but continued to visit me and support me throughout. I was abandoned by my own family.

In 2010, upon my release, I was prevented from travelling down to London on an all expenses paid trip to give a talk on the Southbank in front of leading figures of the Establishment, after winning a national award for poetry, because the police and probation services said I was too dangerous and I might try to contact my ex-Partner again.
My life was subject to a range of constraints and it was impossible to have a normal existence. Once again I was forced to live in a Probation Hostel along with violent criminals, child sex offenders and Rapists. I was recalled to serve yet another year in prison for going on a library computer, even though I had not made any attempt to contact my ex partner, and I had told my probation manager I was doing a job search.
When I returned to prison I was placed on the Main wing. I had young men trying to set fire to my cell and making the most obscene comments and suggestions. Some of them threw urine and semen in a can at me through the door.
I was moved to a Sex Offenders' prison. I asked why I was in a Sex offender's prison when I had not committed a sexual offence, and I was not on the Sex offender's register? A month before the end of my sentence the police came into prison and applied for a SOPO order. They told the Magistrates I was a dangerous Sex offender who was going to attack a member of the general public or my ex girlfriend and commit a very serious sexual offence such as rape (I found that someone in prison had written on my file that I was a 'rapist') as soon as I got released. As a consequence of getting the order they were able to place me on the Sex offender's register for life. I found it very difficult to get anyone to represent me in Court.
The police and Probation dept. sent one of their 'experts' over to interview me. He asked me three questions:
Q. Do you intend to harm your ex girlfriend?
A. No!
Q. Do you intend to hurt either of her children?
A. I wouldn't hurt either of them in a million years. I have told you this a thousand times before.
Q. Do you think you will ever repeat this behaviour with anyone else?
A. I started a friendship with a local businesswoman and ended it when I found she was still in a relationship. She treated me fairly. I stuck to my word, and would never try to force someone against their wishes anyway.
He wrote in his report (for the Court):
*Mr A is a dangerous psychopath who is likely to cause his ex partner or a member of the public serious harm...*

When I came out of prison I discovered that the police had been round
all the people I knew, including my relatives and any prospective
Neighbours.  When I went to my Writer's group the police turned up and
nobody wanted to talk to me even though my sentence was already over.

Even though my sentence was over the police and Probation service
still kept treating me as if I was in prison and kept referring to me as a
Sex offender. In January 2012 I was arrested at the hostel and taken
away in handcuffs. The police accused me of breaking the SOPO
order by going on a social networking site. If I had broken it I would
have been sent to prison for a further five years. It turned out that I
had simply forgotten to log out at the Central library, and someone
had gone on to use my session on the computer.  I week later I was
given permission to go on Social networking sites unimpeded.

I was unable to visit my mother and step-father without the police
constantly turning up to poke their nose in, which meant that I could
no longer visit them. I never received a reply from *Ken Clarke* who was
then trying to reduce the number of detentions in prison.
In order to make a fresh start I tried to get over to Ireland where I had
some relatives. I was stopped and searched before getting on the
ferry, and interrogated at the other side by the police as well, who told me
I was a *Sex offender*, and I would therefore have to sign on and tell
them where I was at all times. All my relatives or associates would also
be informed that I was a dangerous Sex offender.
I returned home from Dublin because I didn't want to
embarrass my sister who is a Drama Teacher, and like the rest of my
family, has never been in trouble in her life.
I told the Irish police that I was not a Sex offender and that I had not
committed a sexual offence.
An officer of the PPU said that if I had not come back they would have
had to spend the year searching for me until I was found.

When I returned I was completely homeless. The Probation
department told the council I had been suitably re-housed (in a hostel
along with violent criminals, serial sex offenders and drug addicts) and
that I had thrown it back in everyone's face.
Their idea was certainly to keep me in the system, shipping me from
hostel to hostel for the rest of my life. I was never able to get a fully
independent assessment done.
I ended up living in an old caravan but was constantly being harassed
by the police. I had rows with them time and time again in front of the
other Residents because they wanted to know what I was doing all the time
and who I was talking to.

I was eventually re-housed by the council due to my poor health.
Even though I had not touched or threatened anyone, or been

convicted of a sexual offence, I had served five years in prison. When I
went to the flat they had found for me I discovered that the police
had been round telling everyone I was a dangerous Sex offender.
When I took my shirt off to sunbathe one nice day the Site Manager
came out to tell me a complaint had been made about me. I spoke
to the Scheme Manager who said that I was perfectly free to sunbathe
in the garden when it was sunny. I asked the Site Manager why she
was so concerned about me sunbathing. She said that I had been in
prison for 'exposure' and that the situation might "escalate."
I made over 35 complaints against the police in 2012, which were
eventually upheld by the IPCC, after the police kept saying it was
nothing to do with them, and invited down to the police station in
Aylsham . I was interviewed by a gentleman who said he had just
changed his job to be head of the investigation unit (but who had been
Head of the PPU-Public Protection Unit who were the exact same
people who had been constantly harassing me and making my life so
impossible). I was interviewed by him with two of the officers who had
been harassing me sat at his side. The police side-stepped all of my
complaints and at the end produced a file about the exposure and
began reading from it. They told me that I didn't like hearing the truth.
I said that I had been charged with breaking a restraining order by
phone contact only over four years ago, and that I was there to
discuss my complaints against them, not about an exposure which was
over and done with years ago.

.

After seeing Anne Owers' (IPCC) staunch defence of the police on
Newsnight a few weeks ago I can quite understand why the police run
rings around us. I have found it impossible to find any work. The police
have appeared whenever I have gone for an interview. I noticed when I
went to sign-on that it said 'Dangerous to women and children, Sex-
offender' on the screen. When I complained and asked them to remove
it they said that they had to listen to a higher authority. This happens
wherever I go. The police are still snooping into my private e-mails and
pestering me all the time.
I am unable to get car insurance and I cannot travel anywhere
without prior notification. A recent change to the law allows the police
to view all my bank statements and all my transactions. I am unable to
put an end to the past.
The police continue to pay me unscheduled visits out of the blue.
Each time I ask them to leave me alone and tell them I have nothing
to say to them. I keep insisting that it has nothing to do with them who
I am seeing. On their last visit they searched through my home taking
photographs, even though I had not broken any laws, and snooped
through all my personal possessions.
They said that they wanted to discuss how many years I was on the
Register for. I showed them the charge form in which it clearly showed
the phone contact four and a half years ago. I told them that it did not

make any mention of a sexual offence. They replied that I had once been convicted of 'exposure.'

I originally wrote to Chloe Smith who said I should write to the IPCC.

My local MP Keith Simpson said that the police are left to deal with Sex Offenders and that he was quite happy with their methods.

I told Mr Simpson that I cannot go on being labelled as a Sex-offender. I cannot get help from a Solicitor because I can't afford a good one and because most Solicitors will not represent anyone labelled as a Sex Offender.

I come from a decent law-abiding family and was educated at a reputable Catholic Grammar School. This is not the kind of life I would have chosen for myself. I have avoided nasty uncouth people all my life.

It is only a matter of time before I have another enormous row with the police at my doorstep. I just wondered if you knew what was going on in this caring and tolerant society we now have....

I am not arguing that my behaviour has been beyond reproach, but that I am underneath a decent caring citizen (if somewhat foolish and prone to risk taking) and that whatever I have done deserves to be treated with some kind of proportionality.

## _Letter sent to Right hon. David Davis MP six years ago._

_No reply._ ^

# BUNTING FAR
BY Crowmarsh Gifford

*Chekov*

## THE WEDDING FEAST AT CANAAN (OR 'MY SECRET JOURNEY INTO MADNESS')

I'm going to try and work a bloody miracle; I'm going to try to make sense of everything that's happened. Not just for you, but for me as well.

There are things which should have been said a long time ago but weren't. Things which were said which shouldn't have been. Nothing I say is meant to embarrass you in any way, but I will have to mention everything which I think is relevant. I just need you to understand the truth and not what people who don't know me have said about me. In all the time I knew you did I ever do anything deliberately to hurt you?

I know you tried to ring me several times, but I just couldn't pick up the phone. I'm not sure why. I never found it easy to talk to you. It just seemed easier to keep you in suspense.

I once gave you a piece of paper with ten things I wanted to discuss with you written down. When I came back from the kitchen it was tossed down the side of the sofa. You said you had read it, but you said nothing. Words are important to me. I prefer to express myself through words.

Some of what you read may be a bit distressing. I am sorry about that, but I just want you to understand what you have done. Some things are very hard to talk about...as time's gone on you must have done a lot of things I haven't been a part of, but there are a lot of questions which still need to be answered. Trying to make sense of the terrible sequence of events may actually make them more bearable. Surely all this suffering can't have been for nothing...?

I may have strained the boundaries somewhat, and I do tend to challenge authority, but I have never been an unpleasant or malicious person. Most things have been as a result of my mischievous nature, my habit of taking risks, my temptation to bend the rules, and to question everything.

I can't begin to say how sorry I am about how things have turned out. I am truly sorry for all the hurt and upheaval I have caused you, but you can't go through the rest of your life believing what is wrong about me. I'm not perfect.

I know I have a devilish streak, and I have done a lot of things I haven't been proud of, but you only have to scratch the surface to find a *Guardian angel*. There are lots of things I would change if I could do.

When I met you I never wanted you to think I was anything other than a decent caring thoughtful gentleman.

Please read carefully what I have to say in private, quietly, without any interference from anyone else.

When we first met you seemed very vulnerable and withdrawn. I drove across in the work van and kissed you through the window (your cheek was very soft). I

recognised your voice from the phone. You were saying goodnight to some
Solicitor friends. I couldn't stay very long. It was already dark.
You complained later about the times I came over. It was quieter in the evenings at
work and it was the only time I could get away.

Another reason is because I find it a lot more peaceful and relaxing after the sun
has gone down and when there aren't a lot of people around.

I contacted you because you lived close by and I felt like some fresh company.
You seemed a bit straight up and down. Not very curvy.

You were very different to anyone I had ever known before.
The second time we met you invited me in and we cuddled on the sofa. You sent me a message on my way across which
read...'in lust...something something:' I thought it was a bit inappropriate. I wasn't really looking for that. Your skin
wasn't like anything I had ever felt before.
You made me a fish curry which was actually very nice even though you refused to believe it.
You made it very obvious what you were looking for and I felt it was my obligation to oblige, but I didn't enjoy any of
it. You made me suck your breasts to see if they were still providing milk. Emily was six, so you would have had to be
doing something unusual for them to go on producing for so long. Anyway, I went along with the occasion, but it all
seemed a bit crazy. You said that you thought Brian had left you because your tummy was too fat. It wasn't that. You
said that you never felt really confident about yourself, so I tried to rebuild your confidence as best I could.
There was nothing I didn't like about you physically, and you did have blue eyes, but there was nothing I felt
particularly attracted to either. You seemed very fragile. You asked me several times: "do you think you could love me,
just a little bit?"
I felt a bit unsure because I didn't know you. You seemed alright.
I thought you had a lovely home, and it was in a nice part of the country. You
seemed to have all the material things in life but very little direction.
You acted as muddled as a hen at a foxhunt. One minute you were a drab
housewife, next minute 'Mother Theresa,' and then a 'craving nymphomaniac.' I wasn't sure what I was doing there or
what I really wanted from you, if anything. You said that when you came back from Saudi and were living in London
you were quite promiscuous and only used men for sex (but not that many!). I tried to make excuses for your
conflicting changes of opinion by saying you were trying to view life from a lot of different angles, but I disagreed
with you a lot about how you went about things. I decided you were totally wrong for me, but that it didn't really matter
because I was never going to stay with you. I told myself that I should never get involved with your family and that
they were incongruous and always bickering.
There is a reason why I never intended to stay which I would like to tell you about...
You asked me if we got along and I said yes. I decided then that I could always
come back to you whatever happened; it was your vulnerability and
craziness...your acceptance, and your gregarious nature.
I went to bed with you without any real desire at all; because you seemed to want
me there. You gave me one of Brian's t-shirts to wear.
You turned up at my place of work early in the morning and shoved a letter
through the letterbox. It was pink and very sweet. You woke me up.

You used to ask me where I was all the time. You sometimes pleaded with me to
let you drive across and stay the night. You seemed desperate not to be left on
your own.
When I rang you from work it was quite funny: "two minutes" – you'd disappear,
and all I could hear for ages was shouting while you put the kids to bed.
You put a lot of pressure on me which I wasn't really prepared for, but I continued
to come round to see you, even though I never felt really sure about my intentions.
I am a very quiet person in spite of my outward appearance, and I'm very shy
sometimes. I don't like a lot of people around.
About three weeks after we had started sleeping together I went to Wales with my

employers. You tried to speak to me every single night. Rose once said to me that she didn't know how you managed to hold down your job sometimes. You were reprimanded for not taking enough time with a patient and for doing your shopping in work time. Rose once asked me if you were still drinking and where you were hiding all the bottles.

I should have been more understanding. I should have been more sympathetic about what you had been through and the stresses on your life. We both agreed that all we wanted was for you to be happy.

Rose said that she and Dennis had been intervening in your marriage and helping to heal the arguments for the final four years.

On the night Brian restrained you and you called the police to have him arrested he said: "there's no way I'm putting this in there!"

No wonder he didn't come back for six weeks.

You said that the reason it had lasted so long was because the sexual side had always worked...sharing confidences and making disclosures to each other is very important too.

I tried to help you but I didn't want to touch you. I don't really know why. I am very sensitive to location and to the situation I'm in.

I once went through your entire wardrobe and drawers. I read everything I could in an effort to understand where I was.

I never saw you wearing anything sexy or seductive.

I watched you go and pay for the petrol in Benson once and watched you walk back. I couldn't see a single thing I desired, which is very regrettable.

Do you remember the flies that summer? They were everywhere. On the ceiling, in the bedroom, on the fly paper. I cleaned the house several times and hoovered them up in thousands from the floor.

We went along to church together for weeks and I met all your friends, even though I had rejected standard Christianity long ago. Then you said you wouldn't go if I was going. Apparently people were asking why we weren't married.

It was a taste of normal family life I had never had. It was sweet to see the children attending their little groups. I suppose it must have happened to me once upon a time....

The first time I started thinking about you was after seeing you trying to play the violin in church. It was hilarious. Very brave!

I remember you calling a dinner party. You invited a lot of your old friends including Justine. She told you that she thought I was very well groomed.

I wasn't really in the mood for socialising but I tried my best for you. They were all nice people and very respectable. Your behaviour was a bit erratic though.

Later in the evening as we were at the table I stood up. It was quite mellow in the candlelight. (I sometimes cooked you a meal, especially if I was off work, for you to come home to).

You suddenly threw yourself onto me and begin crying and kissing my hands. (You have a way of doing this which is quite endearing but too threatening for me).

It was one of the most touching things I remember about you.

I told your friends that I was standing by you. I didn't know if I was your therapist, lodger/housekeeper, or lover....

You invited me to Malta very early in our relationship. I was quite flattered, but I didn't really want to go. I believe that quality time is better spent at home.

I remember walking out on you three times during our relationship. Once was in Malta. I'd had enough of all the children's crying and their spoilt petulant behaviour.

I had been invited on holiday by a work colleague: a big Kenyan girl, who had actually asked me through Pam. I got along with her very well, and she definitely liked me, but I went on holiday with you out of a sense of duty, and feeling I was a member of your family. I asked her what she thought of you after you had come to our barbecue. She said you were very pretty.

I remember that barbecue in the garden especially for one thing. You sat down

on the grass with your legs up a little. I was really shocked to see very bad bruising all over your inner thighs high up. When I asked you about it you said that it had been caused by riding your old bicycle. The only other time I have seen bruises like that was with a girl I taught literacy skills to at the Trust. I saw them one day and wondered if I should report it because I suspected abuse at her home.
I met your aunty, and quite a few of your family. I was struggling to find anything to bond me to you though.

Do you remember going on the giant banana boat in Gozo harbour... and falling off?
Do you still have the pearl earrings I bought you on holiday?
I would have preferred to go abroad on our own rather than with Roger and his screwball entourage. It could have made a big difference.

One of the most enjoyable days I ever spent with you was playing at the side of the river in Wallingford, just beyond the bridge. We played for hours with a burst football, throwing it up in the air and catching it. We pretended to push Benji in and wouldn't let him get out of the water.
We were larking around there all afternoon.
Do you recall sitting on the high bench in the castle grounds? We often went there at the weekend.

I tried to understand you. I thought that one day my feelings might suddenly grow, but I struggled to find a way to connect to you. I even wondered if you had a soul. You seemed to be so disconnected somehow.
I think it's a mistake to think that people have to be very alike to get along though. It may have been my intuition telling me something. From the moment I first drove up to you front door I kept telling myself; if this goes wrong you could end up in serious trouble or you could even die.
I never really committed myself fully to you. I am extremely sorry for being so disingenuous. You must have been very confused.
You once said to me; "You don't come here for sex, so what do you come here for....I don't do a thing for you do I? I can feel it."
I didn't like drinking wine every night, although I often went out to that off-licence in town. They must have got sick of seeing me I went there so many times for you in the evening. Wine gives me a headache. I could quite happily go the rest of my life without a drink. My dad had a bad drink problem and I never wanted to be like him.
I used to check your phone sometimes, and all it had on it were messages from me and Penny...
You said you had fallen out with her, and then I would find you both drinking together in the garden.
I am sorry I used the 'thing' with you. How did I ever sink to that? Some people might see the funny side, but it should never be a substitute for normal loving. I saw you sat up in bed looking at it once. I don't think you really liked it, although you said you knew someone who would. You stripped off on the sofa to use it once. I used to hide it under the stairs. Then it suddenly disappeared. You thought Rose might have found it. How embarrassing...
You pleaded to stay with me at Grays road one night. My laptop was on my bedside cabinet when we decided to watch a film. When I turned it on the most hard-core porn suddenly started playing.
It was a short clip of something which had turned up in my e-mail and I had started watching. I suppose we all get a bit bored sometimes, but I hated to think of you knowing I watched things like that. I remember you sitting up in the bath at Grays road, and me washing your hair for you in your own bath.
I got to the point where I didn't even want to scratch your back in bed. I used to turn over and sleep at the other side. Sleeping has been a big problem for me for years and I fidget like mad sometimes. I don't find it at all easy to sleep when someone else is there. I know you were sad and confused by this. I was very aware of you lying there with your eyelashes fluttering wondering what you should

do. I know you wanted to sleep with your head on my chest but it felt too intense.
You once called out 'help!' You once crept your hand slowly up my leg.
All you wanted was to be close to someone. I am very sorry I found that such a
strain. I like privacy and solitude. I even went to sleep in the spare room
sometimes as Brian had done.
You even found me on the floor in the spare shower-room once.
You started to drink more. I went to the house one evening quite late to find you
in a terrible state in bed. I can't even describe how bad. I don't think it was at all
good for the little ones.

You said: "you're never going to give up your job to be with me!"
You asked me about my bank account and how much I was worth.
I did offer to help you pay your mortgage. I did help where I could.

One evening you had fallen into a coma. I couldn't wake you and I got very
worried.
For ages I just sat and talked to you. I thought that maybe your soul would be
listening to me somewhere. I found it very unsettling and I didn't
really enjoy being with you. I wasn't comfortable.
That didn't stop me from trying to talk to you and spreading little tears over your
eyelids while you were slumbering.  You told me that if I wanted sex I could touch you or
do anything to you, even if you were asleep.  If I could have found a way to find
you more desirable I would have done. I have to apologise for touching you
 inappropriately while you were asleep. It wasn't nice, and it wasn't enjoyable.
While you were asleep on the sofa downstairs once I discovered you were wearing
a pair of black knickers with a huge patch in the crutch which had been frayed to
almost nothing.
You stopped smoking and then you had a fag in your mouth. I hate to see women
smoking. Were you trying to tell me something? You had a hard look, which
alarmed me...I don't know where it came from.
We went out for a meal once with Adam at Waterstones.
It was in the middle of the Michael Jackson court case.

You went off to buy one of his CD's...

When I first met Benji he was on his own. I was shocked by how small and young
he was. He was only seven or eight. I remember what a sweet little voice he had.
I think he knew it as well. He would sit beside me when we played on the
computer or while watching telly. I couldn't understand how he kept beating me
at world cup soccer. I saw you watching us through the kitchen window as we
played at shooting-in on the lawn.
I wanted to teach him so many things. About empathy and trust. How to behave
and how to write.
I went off to buy him a new football down at the shop because he asked for one.

When I came back he just kicked it in the corner. I suddenly realized he had several footballs there already.

I never saw kids with so many bluddy toys and things lying around. Their bedrooms were full of them and they were always getting more.

His leg went a bit septic once, so I went out every day to the chemist to buy him some antiseptic dressing and clean his wound. You wanted me to take him to football practise which I did.

At night he would come and bang on the bedroom door or throw things if he heard a sound. You said he had once walked in on you...

I didn't like the way there was no privacy, and there was a lodger, with people coming and going all the time. The atmosphere seemed strange. Something seemed to be missing...

Then I met Emily.

A bright funny little girl with lots of character.

They reminded me of my sister and me. Both very different but also remarkably similar. The only person who came between us was 'Catty.' It was a bluey-grey colour.

She called it Catty. It had whiskers. It could have been a mouse. She carried it everywhere and would cry if it wasn't there.

Do you remember a little tin doll I gave her on her birthday? She burst into tears when she saw it. It was nice. You laughed at her.

I once brought her some rock back from the seaside. She pranced up the stairs. What a little show-off.

She still trailed around with her dummy in. She was a bit old for one, but it would have been cruel to take it off her. It suited her.

I often read her a bedtime story until she fell asleep. The last story I remember reading to them both was 'the Magician's Nephew' which was one of my old favourites. I'm sorry I never managed to finish it. Roald Dahl's Big Friendly Giant was another one. I read it to them more than once.

You told Penny we were finished, and then she saw us together at the pool.

I remember swinging Emily round in the garden by her ankles and throwing her up high into the air in the swimming pool at the Phoenicia in Valetta. She reminded me of myself in some ways.

The children never seemed to have a proper breakfast. Everything was done at a pace without any real organisation.

I remember putting on her shoes halfway down the stairs one morning....

We were coming back from the fish shop in Wallingford one night. Her tiny little frame was sat in the passenger seat of my Mitsubishi Warrior. I thought it would make a good family car. I remember going to buy it with you.

She suddenly said; "Andrew. Who do you love most. Me or mummy?"

I thought for a while. We weren't getting along too well by this stage.

"I love you both the same but in different ways," I eventually said.

And I always will no matter where she is or how big she gets.

We went to a ballet concert, the first I had every been to, at the little theatre in Wallingford. You were acting bizarrely for some strange reason. If we had been really getting along I would have held your hand all through the performance. It was your behaviour which put me off you. For an intelligent woman you seemed to be so shallow and fickle.

Emily sat on my knee as usual. I wish I could have hugged her more, but she would probably have squirmed and tried to get away.

I leant forward and kissed her little head. You were there. Some of her hairs got stuck to my mouth. She always smelt nice.

She sometimes cheated at cards. I think you should have told her not to do that.

She once pretended to comb my hair....so she obviously had a great sense of humour.

She had a little pound money container. I didn't like you to encourage it, but I didn't have the heart to discourage it either.

After Emily realised Benji could get away with staying in our bed she thought she could too. In the end we all slept together in a heap. I think it's called 'pigging.' It bonded me a lot with you all, and it made me feel left out when I came in at night later and saw you all together.

If I had to leave I always kissed you all before I left. I was just happy for them to be there and I never wanted to push them away or take them anywhere else except their own home.

I don't think it did anything to help our love-life, but it did bring us close together. It gave me a break from the pressure of trying to satisfy you. Who knows. It might have happened naturally one day.

I admit that I have had my problems though.

There isn't anything I wouldn't have done to protect and guard them both from harm. If Emily had been mine I don't think I could ever have left her, and I would have taken her round with me everywhere I went.

No matter how much I loved her, I could never have loved one more than the other. I will never forgive you for turning them both against me and robbing me of their most precious years.

You might think that what happened before we met was not important.

You might wonder why I have to mention these things but I do...!

I met a wonderful attractive lady with reddish brown hair called Mary Holmes (I knew her first as 'Lizzie'). She is the reason why they found the things they did. She was intelligent as well as very beautiful. Some people just have it.

When I went to meet her I always felt happy. A nightingale sung in my heart. When she nestled her head in my lap, just like she used to do with her dad, and I put my arms around her with my head on hers it felt lovely. It felt like true love. One word one message from her and my heart seemed to soar to the Sun.

I only went with her three times and even then I was getting my headaches. I drove halfway across the country to see her and all the time it felt natural. Even if she was asleep she could hear me speaking and would answer me.

The trouble is: every man who met her seemed to feel the same.

She was tall; nearly six foot.

She told me that I was a really nice guy, but that she needed someone to make her feel small. To be honest I do like tall women, but I hate having to stand on tip-toe. I was devastated and felt very ill. My face actually started to swell up.

She'd been married to a six foot five black American basketball player. Her parents had begged her not to marry him, but she said he was unbeatable in bed. She said that marrying him was the worse mistake of her life, yet she said that it would not put her off going with another one.

I decided that it was the last straw. I would do a couple more paintings and make one final collection of poems before ending it all. I still needed to find a way. Then I met you....

I came over to work in Oxford after being offered a really lucrative job with a reputable academic family close by. It also meant that my then girlfriend could visit me more easily. She lived near Coventry and was a Probation Officer. She was very pretty with blonde hair and big blue eyes. We were perfect in every way

151

except one. She was very sociable and relaxed, while I am a hermit who likes to live in a cave.

I am very confident, but I'm also a great perfectionist.

We first met on the train to Oxford, and walked around hand in hand all day. She was a really lovely person, and there was certainly some good chemistry, but even with her I was a complete idiot sometimes and couldn't act normally. She put up with it for a long time though. I think she really cared for me and she didn't want to see me get hurt. After we went to Florence together I checked her e-mail and found out she had been with an ex boyfriend just after we had a slight tiff. Unbeknown to me he had been pestering her for months.

I just knew something was wrong: apart from me I mean. We were about to take a bus trip around Florence and we climbed on board. She sat half-way down the bus. I walked all the way down to the back. She started crying....

I carried her little picture around in my pocket and slept with it under my pillow for over a year...

I was five years old when I first saw Lydia. She had just started school. I remember her being brought into our classroom and blushing near the door just as I had done. I loved her all the way through school.

When I was eleven my mum and dad were going through a very unhappy divorce. My dad used to get very violent when he had been drinking, and a lot of it was directed towards me.

We were in the top class, and due to leave. We were due to go to different schools. I remember agonising for months how to tell her how I felt but never did even though I saw her looking at me sometimes.

I was sixteen when I saw her walking with her sister down the street. She lived on the next street to my uncle and grandmother. Everyone could see that she was pregnant. I knew from that day that I could never ever be happy. When I was about forty-three someone sent me some details from a dating agency. I rang the owner and managed to get her phone number. The woman who answered could have been my Lydia. She talked about her family having to flee Eastern Europe at the beginning of the last war. I wrote a long letter to her, and only at the end did I tell her about the girl I used to know. I was working down in Kent at the time.

She rang my mum wanting to speak to me. She wrote a very sincere and heartrending letter all about her life.

She spoke about a toy soldier I had given to her in the school playground when I was eight. It had been very important to me but I had forgotten all about it. She also brought back other memories I had forgotten (and I thought I had a good memory). She spoke about a little boy at school who was like her in every way. She said: "Andrew, we all have problems, just different ones!"

"The soul is immortal, and lives far beyond this space and time."

She said: "this is the love I would have always wanted..."

I found her very deep and moody though. She warned me about how hurtful she could be...Lydia was still living with someone in a large house on the outskirts, but they were getting divorced she told me.

She would ring me in the middle of the night and beg me to take her away.

I had her in bed several times but I just couldn't find any desire.

When I couldn't or wouldn't make love to her she burnt all my letters and sent them back to me in the post...

When I opened her letter I could feel my heart stop beating.

That's the first time I ever thought about ending my life.

You once said that you had done when Brian left.

As you know, I once worked for the Samaritans.

I managed to persuade a gangster in Chicago to send me a revolver disguised as automobile parts. I told him it wasn't to hurt anyone else, but that I knew someone who wanted to end their own life. It was nothing to do with me hurting anyone else: it was about being a failure and worrying about growing old. Too many things had gone wrong to mention. I was close to someone in my early twenties,

but lost her. He said he would send me ten bullets to practise with. I had no idea
what dum-dum bullets were or how to fire a gun. I wasn't even sure what a firing
pin was. He said that he didn't know if it would be any good to me...
I tried to contact him again because it kept falling apart and seemed to be
welded in the middle but his phone didn't answer.
It had a swastika on it, and appeared to be from the First World War, a Browning
revolver, with 'museum de Belgique' stencilled on it....
I was scared to go near it and kept moving it about from place to place.
I told myself that I would not change my mind.
That was when I met you. The gun was nothing to do with you. It was a silly idea:
although we all have to die some day, and I would rather it was quick. My
stepfather was dying of cancer and is still suffering today.
I should have thrown it away or just talked to someone about how I was feeling.
You knew something was wrong but I didn't think you would be able to cope
with what I told you. Quite understandably you would have been very worried
about me. I bottled it all up every night and that is why I behaved like I did.

That is why, even when you were doing your best to love me, even when you were
following me around all weekend so I didn't abuse myself and flooding me with
affection, I couldn't open up and say anything.
I must say I have always been a bit of clown. I have played a number of practical
jokes over the years, but nothing as bad or as serious as the ones which followed.
Benji had gone to his friends in Eyam when I decided to close the place I had
been renting in Wymondham. It was costing me a fortune, and I was hardly ever
there. We went across to pick up all my things with Emily.
You made me call at my mums, but they were out. I wonder if that would have
changed anything, if you had met. Keith had to go to hospital.
I really regretted Benji not being there. My mum would have loved him. She
would have really spoiled him. I greatly regret him missing her, because I think he
would have loved it too. My mum has a great way with children.
I remember getting some fresh prawns and going down to the beach in
Sheringham. You were really annoying me and I was ready to finish with you when
we got back. I suppose I must have appeared very grumpy and bad tempered. I
couldn't sleep and I felt unhappy and under a lot of pressure.
Emily changed on the beach and went to splash in the sea. She was very funny
and loved every minute of it. I went in as well.
I got some paint things out at the house to give her something to do. I still have a
painting she did.
I am really sorry I couldn't be more normal with you. I am really sorry I worried you.
I was horrible to you, and you didn't really deserve it. You were still very loving.
Your attitude was strange. I didn't feel any connection with you and your ways.
You once said that you were even more sensitive than me.
I drove back as quickly as I could. When we got near home you said; "Can't you
drive any faster?"
I told you that you should be more loyal to people. I am sorry I ignored you for
most of the journey.
When I returned to Grays road you sent me a message to say you didn't want to
see me any more. I couldn't have blamed you, but after all the attention you'd
given, if anyone was going to finish with anyone it was going to be me!
I went round to Rose and Dennis's. I couldn't believe it when he told me to go
away or he would call the police. I thought he was being a very horrid little man.
When I eventually found you we made up and I stayed the night again.
I might have been a lot closer to you than I thought.
I helped you with repairs and did all sorts of chores which needed doing
around the house. You said that Brian had never bothered.
<u>Property</u>
When we returned from Norfolk I put some of my possessions into the garage, and
some in the house. These included:
☐ A brand new large screen TV

☐ Some of my favourite DVD's
☐ A brand new hi-fi (which resided under the fish tank)
☐ A new DVD recorder
☐ A brand new mountain bike for you to use in place of your old one (we went out sometimes on the bikes at weekends in an effort to get you fitter or did some running on the hill)
☐ A new web-cam
☐ I left some of my best CD's in your stack and I bought you some new ones

I did a small watercolour which you hung above the fish tank...behind it I stuck a note :- 'you gave me a dream of a happy home and family, something I never really had, and I gave you this little picture, which I mistakenly thought would be my last'

I left a large picture of you. I think I had your face brilliant at one point, but I took it a bit too far as usual...
I left you a selection of books...
In one of the books I wrote - 'for Benji and Emily - I love you both....'

## Car boot sales

We did a few car boot sales together, mainly at the Kassam.
Do you remember me in the back of the pick-up giving away almost everything I owned for next to nothing? Bottles of wine, mini TVs - everything. I sold a lot of other things when you weren't there. You went off to get some drinks and a bacon sandwich with the kids. I think some items were stolen because I couldn't keep my eyes on everyone.
You looked puzzled and a little confused.
 You kept wondering why I was giving away all my worldly goods, well now you know....!
You told the fuzz I had sold everything I had at the sales.
You even betrayed me with your neighbours.
That dog of theirs was like Sherlock bloody Holmes; always picking up my scent.

### Internet dating

I had relationships with a lot of different women from all around the world while living in Oxford. I saw the way people went from one partner to another all the time, and I never wanted you to do the same. It seemed such a waste of time and effort. I think the best relationships develop and deepen over time.
You told me you had met about two people between Brian and me.
One was a vicar with funny shoes, and the other one worked in a supermarket at Didcot (I found a message from him saying he had to go home but that he didn't want to). You told me you didn't want to see him but he kept pestering you?
Just before you I met Honor. She mixed with some of the Royal family and her family owned land all over the place, with a restaurant in Italy. I'd seen it all before we met. She was very into exhibitionism, which I really wasn't.
She brought a lot of presents when she came over including wine and cheeses. She gave me a little handmade bible which she had been given in Mexico. She had written 'I love you' inside.
Honor was very bright and sensual, but we were like chalk and cheese

When I came home one day you told me you had been with three different men that week while I was away.
*You told me that you wished the sexual side had worked better in our relationship because it would have brought us a lot closer together.*
When I checked your phone and e-mail it appeared to be true.
One of the messages said; 'right thing wrong time, I enjoyed it too!'
You said that you had only just met one of them on the street. I was under a lot of pressure at the time. I would like to tell you why. I still didn't want to touch you. You told me that you wouldn't be bothered if you went with five different men in a week.  Before it had been only me.

154

You told me one of them was only interested in sex.
You said that you wouldn't mind using the internet for sex.
I told you I didn't want to lose you.
I didn't know what to say or what to believe.
You said I already had.

You said you were going to marry someone called Dave.
You said you could feel it.
I said, "but you haven't even met him yet...!"
It was all very confusing. I didn't know what to do.
Then you told me that you thought you might have dreamt it all...
I had wondered about some kind of threesome to get me interested. I once left
Rachel a note near the washing machine one night. She sometimes came down
to unlock the door for me. It was very brazen.
You were snoring away upstairs. I asked her if she wouldn't mind coming and
sucking on your breasts for half an hour....
I couldn't believe it when she thought for a while, and then said ..."Oh, alright!"
I didn't take her up on it and left soon after, but your voice sounded a bit quaky
when I spoke to you on the phone the next day.
I came back one night and you told me to go away or you would call the police.
I had a key cut when you left me to go off to work.
When I went back the next night you asked me if I would be staying all week.
You were in a terrible state. I had a pretty good idea you had been with
someone. I still felt nothing except confusion: no feelings. I told you that you
didn't have to behave like that.
You were lying in Emily's bed when we started petting.
You told me David had brought an overnight bag the first time you met. You went
to pick him up at Cholsey station. I've hated the place ever since.
The men you went with all seemed to fizzle out. You told me that you might have
sex with me next, or it could be someone else.
I thought your behaviour just wasn't right.
Your tongue was wagging about as I looked down on you in the light from the
doorway.
"If you could make love with anyone in the whole world who would it be?" I asked.
You hesitated a second and said...
"You?!"
What can I say?
Your craziness was exasperating. Perhaps I had started to care about you. It's the
one thing I do miss a bit.
The love I had only felt in your hands started to come back again. Perhaps you are
a Healer like me...?
I woke up one night with you feeling the top of my head. You shot back. Bound
to be curious I guess. I wasn't angry. It was quite sweet.
Then one night your arm suddenly flopped over me.
You laughed when I made a funny sound in bed.
We started having sex during one of your periods and I got your blood all over
me...another time I found you wearing knickers in bed.
You asked me if I would be taking my things when I went.
I left them because I always thought I would come back...
And I never wanted you to forget me.

## AN INCIDENT

In August something really bad happened. You kept asking me what was wrong.
You said there was something wrong. *You told me about a dream you had. You
had gone somewhere to see me. Some of your friends were there. The flatfoots
were there too, but they wouldn't let you into the building.* It was a stupid petty
little business, which was blown right-out-of-proportion. I was struggling to know
what to do with you.  I was bored and fed-up. My life just didn't feel at all happy,
and I wasn't cut out for balloon dancing.

I didn't do anything sexual. I suppose I just like to shock people sometimes. I really should know better. It was a very silly thing to happen. All it brought me was misery. I told you that I'd had an argument with someone in town. I was very ashamed of letting you down.

I called in a shop on the High street and started trying on clothes. One of the assistants came back with a pair of trousers and when she handed them over through the changing room curtain she saw that I was only half dressed, and that was all. She turned and walked away without reacting. Two to three seconds at most.

The Assistants could be seen acting out what had happened on the shop video. I walked calmly out of the door.

No matter what you think about these things, it certainly doesn't deserve the title 'Sex-offender,' and I did not deserve the awful repercussions which followed.

It wasn't something I could really talk to you about even though you ran a clinic on sexual health.

The Authorities must have known about me and you. I am surprised they didn't come rushing around to tell you bad things about me then.

Shortly after it happened you were leaving work and the miserable toads fined you for not wearing your seat belt.

About three weeks after the original incident I cycled into town down Headington hill and saw there were people in plain clothes *and* uniforms all around.

When I came out of Boots the chemist four officers jumped me and dragged me in handcuffs through the crowded streets to the main police station. I decided to plead guilty to exposure and wrote the manager of the shop a letter of apology. I just couldn't face a lengthy court case.

I was held for ten hours while they played their pathetic games.

Poor Adam was at home wandering what had happened to me.

I spoke to Pam on the phone about what had happened. She was very understanding. I sent her a text saying that no-one love me.

She said that lots of people did.

Pam said I ought to tell you myself what had happened rather than you hear it from someone else. We weren't getting along too well. Even if it had been months before I would have found it hard to tell you.

You had just started your course at the college.

I needn't remind you that it was my idea that you did Osteopathy. You weren't happy in your job. I suggested it because I had a friend called Clare Farleigh who had gone on to do it after nursing.

I came up to see you. You were parked outside. You drove off.

You said that love had to come from both sides. What a bluddy cheek!

You'd started asking me if we were better just being friends. I recall going up the hill to the garden centre. What a cold mood you were in. I was really fed up with you.

I was there one night when you said you were expecting an important phone call or two. You had been away all weekend and your phone was switched off.

When I turned up and asked you where you had been you asked me what I was doing there. You flinched when I touched you. The first time I felt a twinge of desire you pushed me away.

You said you had stayed one night with Karen, and one night with your brother's friend. His wife didn't really like you staying. He was black I think. You said he had been suspended from his job in the Health service for a suspected sexual assault. You said he once made a pass at you.

You told me your breasts were sore because I had sucked them too hard.

When the phone rang you closed the door.

I sat on the sofa in the lounge and tried to hear what you were saying. It all sounded very deep and emotional. Your voice went quite high some of the time.

You said to whoever it was: "We are friends, aren't we?...you are the best friend I have ever had."

"Friends, yes! Yes I know you are having trouble with you wife..."

You looked quite secretive and cold when you returned.
Pam once asked me why I always seemed to meet such needy women.


For weeks I had deliberately stayed away or went off somewhere else. I am a strange man
sometimes I know. I had a special cake made for your birthday, and I made you a card with a
poem I'd written inside.
I also ordered you a large bouquet of flowers in Wallingford.
I went out to Woodstock shopping for you and found a brown fur jacket top. I got you a size too small.
She said I could bring it back if it was too small.
These I presented to you on your birthday.
I just turned up at the house like before.
You said that Penny had invited you out but that you would rather stop in with me.
You wore your new top, even though it was a bit of a squash. I am so sorry for
that. I never got chance to change it for the right size.
I never got to taste any of that lovely cake either...
On Sunday you invited me to help you at Emily's birthday party.
Dennis was surprised to see me at the hall. We made friends. He'd had a lot of
trouble with his eyes I think...
I helped to pay for the venue as you didn't have enough money.
It was a nice day and I remember us taking pictures of Emily running across the hall. She was in her element.
I felt very tense. You pushed me away when I touched you which wasn't very nice and you made fun of me.
Rose noticed how you were treating me.
The clown said he thought I was with Rose. Not very complimentary, but you did say Brian had a nice face.
That night I read Benji his story in bed as usual, but I had a splitting headache.
You asked me if I would be staying, but I had to get away to bed.
In the morning I appeared in Court all by myself.
I did my best, but still received a hefty fine.
What was even worse: they put me on the Sex offender's register for five years. It
meant that the police would be calling round and interfering in my life. I also had
the Probation department ringing my employers and trying to cause trouble.
I had just got back from Court when I received a text message from you. I could
have done with all the help I could. I have never been sure to this day whether
the police came to see you and tried to say the most nasty and unpleasant things
about me.
Your text message said: 'I don't want to see you again. No further contact.'
My care of Adam was affected by what was going on and I greatly regret that.
I think that if he had ever seen you he would have run you down in his wheel chair.
Adam never knew about the Court case. He would have been too upset.
I still came round as you know. I didn't know what to say to you.
I sent you a text message. I was used to you being there.
You replied with the only truly hurtful message I have ever received from you;
'I don't know you!'
That is so true really. I never let you get to know me because I was never sure
about you or the future.
I felt guilty that you had known me for eight months, during which time we had
slept together on and off, and I had never let you into my heart or confided in you
about anything which really mattered or which had altered my life...


I cycled all the way from Oxford just to look in the drive. I even saw Benji and Emily
taking Fluffy out for a walk one morning, but I couldn't go near you.
On one occasion Benji came running from his friends to talk to me. He thought I
was coming in, but I told him to go back.
Another time he actually blushed.
There was an occasion a few months later when you had a college teacher with
you all morning: a Friday I think.
Benji: "I've just seen Andrew!"
You: silence....then "Where was he?"
Benji: "Just outside..."

After your friend had gone...

You: "Did you really see Andrew? What did he do?"

Benji: "He just went away!"

You: "Don't talk to him!"

Benji: "Why not?"

"Why do you think...!?" you snapped.

You might wonder how I know all this...?

I looked at you one day, and decided you would be the wrong person to joke with.

You *said* I would see a different side to you.

You were in the kitchen with Sandra.

Let me tell you something about Sandra. I don't think she's had it as easy as you might think. You were always sensitive about her. Yes, I saw she was beautiful, but there is no way I could ever have touched her instead of you.

I sent you a message about wizards. It was only meant as a bit of light-hearted banter.

You replied (with Sandra): 'go and see a doctor. You are sick!'

And 'fuk off you impotent loser!'

If you thought things like that would hurt me you are very much mistaken, but you obviously thought they would hit me where it hurt. I thought they were very childish and petty comments to make, and they say a lot about the kind of person you are.

I was shocked that you could send messages like that though.

By the way. I never sent you twenty messages a day. You were lucky if you got one or two.

I once rode past you on the field. You were standing with your arms round Emily.

*The reasons I came back and what I did there:*

I came back because, strange to say it, I actually missed you, and it felt like home...

I had often left in the middle of the night to get some sleep.

I had often turned up late because that was the only time I could get away and because I liked to read their bedtime story and tuck you all in.

One day you stopped right next to me in the car at the traffic lights. Emily stared at me through the window and seemed very puzzled. I was staying in a hotel down the road at great expense.

You were on the computer with them one night. You talked to them about the devil's number. You had obviously discussed it with them before.

I wonder what they will think of you when they get older?

I sent you a message at most once a month, but each time I did I was there watching you in the garden.

Maybe I just like spying on people. I do like finding out about people's little secrets. It was a teeny bit creepy!

I wanted to see your reaction and I actually learnt a lot more about you during this time. You once tracked your ex all the way to Spain (the German guy who you met as his nurse in hospital) and groped his partner. You said there was nothing there (she had a flat chest). So you know all about this kind of behaviour?

You once said to me: "You wouldn't ever hurt me if we fell out would you?" What a silly question to ask! It was almost as daft as asking me if I would touch either of your children. Not in a million bluddy years! I thought it was stupid and insulting.

I saw you in the restaurant we used to go to, with Mat R.

He didn't take his glasses off even when you massaged his back.

You kept referring to me as 'the nutter.' Thanks!

I saw you take out the photograph album when he had massaged your chest.

You touched his leg.

I watched for a few moments. It was so boring. I felt a bit sorry for both of you and went home.

You left his address at the side of the sofa. He used you just for the night and you had probably done likewise.

I spoke to him disguised as another woman on-line.

He bragged about fking you listening to the BG's on my hifi.

I woke about ten the next morning with a horrible impression. I could feel and hear what you were doing. It was truly awful. I could hear you saying ouch...he bragged about a...l intercourse. What on earth were you doing letting him do that to you!? I could hear a lot of panting and grunting.

He didn't come back. He must have been quite sane after all.

The next time I saw you after Christmas you looked awful...your hair was very bedraggled and you looked pale and drawn. You looked very upset and unwell.  It may have been me. You reported me for leaving some poetry in a drawer, and a Christmas card on the wall.


I was out in the garden when I sent you one of my rare messages. I was watching you carefully, but I couldn't go across or do anything.  The paper with his address and phone number was still at the side of the couch.

I texted you: 'I miss U' - that was all.

I saw you read it and nod your head. You started crying and touched your face. I am so sorry for any pain I have caused you....

I left you a bottle of wine sometimes and other things as well. I wrote a note on the back of my kitchen board until you took it down.

 It was the one with a duck on the front, which had hung on my kitchen wall for years.

I thought it was especially funny to write notes in your Calendar, like 'apologise to Andrew'...(in December).

I am a very sentimental person really. I thought that one day you would understand me better.

A WPC I met at a party in Southampton advised me not to have anything more to do with you. She warned me you were trouble and to keep away from you. She said you were the one with the problem.

I remember Howard insisting: "She's reported you once. She'll do it again!"

He was furious about my antics.  You had once sat down in his chair.

I deliberately set you up with a black guy called Massi to see how you would react. It was a silly thing to do. I gave him your name on 'lovenfriends.'

He was nasty piece of work. He went around seducing white women on line and then he would display the pictures he took, so everyone could see.

I used to read your e-mails between each other. He contacted you under two different names. In one he pretended to be white.

The last thing I knew about him he was living in Croydon.

I once rang him to find out about you but he was very slippery. Not even my private detective friend could get him to say a thing.

His usual voice-mail message said: "life is a box of chocolates. You never know what you are going to find...."

I put a photo of you up on line a few months later. He obviously recognised you, and seemed to know a lot about you. He said he wanted to meet someone who was passionate, very sexual, and could keep a secret. He also said he was into Dildos and oral sex. He told me that he had never visited Oxford.

You told him that I had put a picture which looked like you on-line...

(A man listed as living at your address but also with a business address in Oxford called Calvin Shields sold marital aids and sex aids on the Internet).

You told a policewoman who called at my place of work that I had put your details on line because someone told you.

One evening before you met Kevin you dressed yourself in black with little ringlets in your hair I had never seen before, and were gone all night.

You looked a bit the worse for wear the next day, but not as bad as before. Your hair looked a bit matted.

In 2006 you sent me a sexually explicit voice-mail message when you thought it was Massi who had texted you. You said that you had once had an incredible sexual experience in your car and that you hoped he would respond. I think you were a bit drunk to be honest.  There's a turn up for the book!

I am sorry for playing these silly games with you. It would take a lot of explaining...

I was very unhappy when I saw you meeting regularly with Kevin Br. Naturally I read all your messages. It lasted a lot longer than I thought it would. I saw Roger in Wallingford. He told me that he was alright but that he wasn't used to dealing with children. I was there the first night you introduced him to the kids. You kept going back to see how they were getting on.

I heard you telling someone on the phone that all Kevin did was stuff himself with cream cakes all day and talk about his ex wife.

You told them that he certainly wasn't the one for you.

You actually described him as 'sweet!'

I went in once when he had hurt his foot and couldn't visit you that weekend. He preferred to go out with the boys then anyway, he said.

You were in a poorly state in the small room at the front. You had made it into a little bedroom. I felt really sorry for you, and went close to you a few times but was frightened to wake you up because I wasn't sure how you would react. You seemed so lonely and alone.

I hated you making fun of me with the kids and their friends.

I hated you playing games at the window and kissing him when you thought I was outside.

I hated seeing his car there, seeing him pawing at your chest, attempting to kiss you, wiping his saliva away, lying on his chest, slopping wine.

I wanted it to end....I thought that I would forgive you though.


I found Massimo's details on your phone when I came in one night.

You saw me once in the garden, I think, I don't know how. You went on the phone. I was questioned by a police car which suddenly appeared from nowhere on the High street.

I went back and saw you were absolutely paralytic.

You were on the sofa all alone and looking very unhappy.

I looked at you and said out loud from the garden: "I love you!"

It was as if you could hear me.

The reaction from you was very upsetting.

You burst into tears like I had never seen before. They were rolling in big lumps down your cheeks and you were sobbing. You started nodding your head exactly as I said it.

You got up after a while but you were very rocky and fell, breaking a glass. Fluffy was petrified.

As you lay on the floor he was meowing loudly in consternation.

I let myself in and cleaned up the glass, then I lifted you up onto the sofa and covered you with a blanket, and then left. I think Kevin had gone to bed to sleep off the booze.

I was there the first night that Yas stayed. I thought he looked Chinese.

He kept dusting the side of the sofa. You were upstairs, and when you came down you had a lot of eye makeup on. You kept licking your lips. He had gone upstairs by then. He seemed a pleasant enough fellow. He told you that relationships were never equal. He said Kevin looked like a used car salesman. Yas was always looking for more from you. Originally you told him: "friends, just friends, yes?!"

Yas started coming across on a Friday at a time when Kevin wasn't coming as often. I heard you in the garden begging Kevin not to go, just as you had done with me.

He came round for the last time at Christmas. You kissed him at the doorstep.

I came back to see Fluffy, sit him on my lap, talk to him, feed him, and clean his tray, which was really disgusting sometimes.

I mended your door which was sticking.

I checked my property and your phone. You left it out in the garden more than once.

I put the boot down on your car because you had left it open all night and it was blowing in the wind.

I took some milk to make a drink.

I used to come in late at night and look at you in bed with Benji and Emily holding you on either side. I turned the light off once and you woke up. You must have known it was me. You said to Anna: "It's my Stalker. He comes in at night, but I don't think he's dangerous."

I left some chocolates in your coat pockets (which I believe you handed round to friends) – they came to interview me about them as you know because Debbie G. showed you my book. Didn't you ever see the advert...Cadbury's milk-tray? I didn't even know it was a crime.

 I was in and out like a jack-in-a-box one night. You were lying in bed. They should have been there, but I couldn't see them anywhere. You were all alone I think. It was now or never. God, did the floor in your bedroom creak. Back and forth like a yo-yo. Eventually I leaned over and kissed you ever so lightly on your forehead. You stirred and moaned a little. I was scared what you might do if you saw me. It was the first time I had touched you in months. It was very tender. I turned and walked carefully away...

On your 43rd birthday you must have been out somewhere. You were dozing on the downstairs sofa. Your face looked a little thinner. I wondered what it had been through since we were friends. I didn't touch you. I just stood there looking. Your dress was rucked up and your nylons all hanging down. I felt quite sorry for you. I went and found some flower petals and scattered them in your lap. I didn't dare leave any obvious evidence of my visit because I didn't want any more pigs embarrassing me at work.
 I left you a bottle of wine.
I took a pair of your used knickers (to my surprise they were very intoxicating).
I left two little jugs. You kept some papers in one. I heard you say to Rose; "I don't know where that came from!"
I made them myself in a kiln nearby....
I played tricks on you with the keys. I sometimes took them from your keyring and had them for all the doors. I thought I had lost the front door key once so went in and took the only one you had. I am extremely sorry for that. I heard you outside trying to get in. You had to go round to Rose's. I heard Benji and Emily sighing; "locked out of our own home!"
I left a little bonnet I had bought at the British library for Emily. I hope she wore it.
I left your Christmas presents.
I checked my note to see if it was still there, and when it wasn't replaced it with a carbon copy (as you know!).
I wrote in your address book.
I signed you up to an internet telephone account and monitored your calls.
I twiddled with my thumbs and wondered what to do.
I used the loo, or had a bath.
I read all your post.
I changed some of the labels on your Osteopathy skeleton.
I went to the garage.
I moved your vase. The one you had tried to hide behind when Yas was there.
I turned your bedroom light on and off.
I went through your drawers.
I left a photo in one of my psychology books.
I asked myself various questions, like;
Do you think this is bordering on obsession.
What if she finds out...
What is going to happen?
How do you think this is all going to end?
I just didn't want you to forget me! As if you ever could.
I kept a large notebook of my activities. It was really just a wind-up. I kept it out of boredom. I needed something to occupy my mind.
I have always liked writing.
A chap called Shane rang you. He arranged to meet you while you were out at Dennis's. He was from Mauritius. He told me you were keen on his nationality but you weren't sure about him being follically challenged and over fifty. If I remember rightly you said that anyone who wasn't married and hadn't had kids by the age of fifty wasn't fit for anything. You left his details in the cat basket. Then you met Danny. He was the one with the piggy-eyes. You told him about me, and went to the pub up the hill. The one we used to go to on a Sunday. You

both looked at the sidewall when you drove in the cul-de-sac. He started groping your chest on the sofa. Not again I thought.

By that time Yas had gone up to bed. You left him in the house by himself. He appeared content to step aside but you could tell what he was thinking and where he wanted it to lead.

You were dressed in your usual red cardigan when you went out with Danny that night, and you had applied a lot of make-up. When you came back your face was very pale and you looked terrible. All your make-up seemed to be gone. When Danny started groping you seemed very nervous, but still flung your head in his lap. It all seemed so unreal. As if you were just acting a part.

Yas went to the upstairs window and looked out into the garden. I thought he might have seen me dashing across.

You were quiet the next night and sat with your back to the window. You looked a bit self-conscious talking to Yas and Anna.

Yas liked it better when it was just you and him. He joked about having to lock his door at night, and paying you in sex instead of board.

You glared for a long time on your own...

"Friends, just friends!" you said. You took it in turns to go on-line. You told Jo you had spent the last four days together.

You read him Kevin's e-mail when he finished with you. Kevin said he had wanted to finish with you before but he couldn't because Alex was there.

I sent you a message about having your back scratched.

Yas told you that you if you scratched someone's back they would have to do the same for you.

I recall him pretending to expose to you, and playing games at the bathroom window.

You told him about the church in London and your friends there.

You bragged to him about you being a Scorpio.

That night you sat there applying makeup and doing your nails. You kept on applying lip-gloss, as he sat behind you....I couldn't see if he was touching you or not....your eyelids began flickering nervously, then you looked very worried and self conscious, then you looked very hard and a bit upset and got up. You went back to the computer. He castigated himself, as if he had missed his chance. You both kept on going to the bathroom.

The next message I sent you was a bit of tease.

I said that you were bound to turn someone on if you had your white breasts and pink nipples sucked.

You told Yas I was your Stalker, and that you couldn't stand me. I heard you saying the same thing about him on the phone.

You sent me a message with him and asked for his help. It said;

'squishy little pink dick' and (once more) the well worn 'fuk off u impotent loser!' He was quite submissive most of the time.

I went in one night and heard you open your door and pretend to scream to see if he would come to your room.

Sandra asked you if he smelled.

When you showed him a picture of Danny. Not a very attractive person by all accounts, Yas said, "well maybe he has a big dick?"

You replied: "I don't like it when you talk like that!"

All this seems so familiar.

You asked him if he found you 'boring.'

You sat there on the couch, almost laughing, playing with your bra-strap, sneaking a look at his face. You even had Anna in on the act one night, while I was freezing out in the garden....

I left a poem about Fluffy for Benji. You took it down after a few weeks.

Apparently Emily found it and wouldn't go in the Wendy house again.

I don't know why but Yas seemed to have decided to keep himself to himself. You asked him if he would like to go on holiday to Malta: "I'm on my own and so are you. The kids would love it!"

162

He asked you to ask him again in the middle of the week when you were more sober.
You asked him if he would like to start a business in Malta...
He said it didn't matter if you were 42-3 and he was 27?
You told him that you couldn't give him any children though...
Anyway he suddenly got up and went to bed.
You sat there for ages by yourself, licking your lips and fantasizing. Putting your hair
up, and letting it down again. Then you fell over spilling your glass.
I don't know what happened when you eventually went up to bed, but I got
bored of sitting around and trying to stand in that little infant chair.
The next night your face was very flushed as you rushed around his bedroom
changing the bed sheets...
The next weekend Yas was there with Anna. Benji was on the Osteo couch. He
was stroking his head and talking to him the way I used to do.
You were a little the worse for wear, but went in the kitchen and started talking to
Anna. You told her that he was 'very sexual' and that you had had sex.
The next night you were by yourself at your computer touching yourself.
A strange thing happened while I was at my caravan round the corner doing your
portrait. I put your picture next to a decent picture of me to see what we looked
like together. It was very sad to see: we might have been a lot closer than I
imagined. I couldn't wait any longer:
I sent what I believed to be my final book of poetry to your father (and I thought
you were mad!).
As a Professor of Literature I thought he would preserve my work and when I was
dead appreciate my sincerity.
You were down in Wales going through my book the next weekend...
When you came back you took down my picture again because of something I
had written and left it on top of the table...I wasn't going to put a message behind
it a third time if that's what you were thinking!
I once spoke to your father about Shakespeare. He was sat on the purple sofa in
the living room. He wanted to know how I could quote from every tragedy.
When your parents visited I acted normally and tried to get on with them both.
Even though you said your mother was a bitch I was determined to give them a
chance and treat them both with respect. I tried not to be distracted by the story you
told me about your dad getting down in front of a car to stop you going to
church. I can get along well with anyone who likes words and literature.
I thought you took after him quite a bit in other ways.
I never noticed your mum's legs. She is quite old. I found her to be more sensitive
than you made out.
 Your father kept ruffling his head and looking at me. Never seen a bald one before....
I never made a proper effort to dress up smartly and conduct myself in the way I
know I can. It was because I had given up on life.
 I used to leave my shoes and clothes at the side of the bed, and they were always
still there the next time I came.
We had a meal with your mum and dad at the table. I think Sandra was there too.
I was interested to discuss religion with them. Your mum appeared to be a very
traditional Catholic and a monarchist.
I even stood up for your mum a bit when you began putting her down. That is why
I was a bit disappointed when you told me she said I "wasn't presentable" - a
doctor or a barrister like your brothers.
I didn't sell myself or make myself presentable. That was my frame of mind and I
am very sorry for my failings.
She said she had only put up with your ex husband for your sake.

Pam once said of you that I 'could do a lot worse....'
When you came back from visiting your mum and dad the police tried to talk to
me but I ignored them. I could feel your mother's thoughts.
She must have read some of my book- 'small bird's sing.' It needed some more editing.
I think she felt a bit sad about what was happening.

Adam had suddenly died. You remember stopping at his house and meeting his family...? He had suffered a huge aneurism in his head.
I was at his bedside holding his toe when he slipped away. I had brought down all his cuddly toys to put round him at the John Radcliffe: his brown bear, his giraffe, and his blue sea-lion.
I sent you a message from his bedside. His sister was in tears.
You replied: 'fuk off, or u r nicked!'

You were lying on the sofa by yourself. I think you knew I would be round. I just wanted to put my arms round you and make everything alright, but I just couldn't do it. I was scared of someone coming down. The light was on in the bedroom even though it was very late. I went in and out several times, before I suddenly saw Benji at the top of the stairs looking down. He came down a step or two. I would have loved to reassure him, but I simply shut the door and went away. I went back to see him trying desperately to wake you up. His face was pouring with tears, poor lad. What did I ever do to make this happen. What did I ever do to make this poor little boy who I had carried in my arms to bed each night so afraid? I knew it was bound to happen one day after several close escapes.
You even came down one night in your blue nightie and missed me by a whisker.
One time you sat with your head on the kitchen table. I couldn't have done this to anyone else.
It was you! Telling them stories. My behaviour was very silly, but I certainly didn't mean any harm. I wouldn't have hurt him for the world or harmed a single hair on his head. I wouldn't have hurt any of you in a million years, but I have been labelled along with the very worse type of people despite my saying this over and over again.
 If only we had been able to talk instead of you sending silly messages and shaking your head. You were sitting there one night all alone and crying. You were wearing a pullover I had given you which my mum had knitted. I sent you a tease -"that's my mother's woolly pullover you're wearing...!"
It was very touching seeing you in it and it made me cry.
You told Penny about my message...
She replied: 'scary-call the police!'
You told me Penny could be very two-faced.
The next night you locked the front door.
The night after that you didn't.

# Crime and Punishment

I had just been to Adam's funeral. There were some lovely people there. It was all very emotional.
I'd had my caravan on the site just round the corner for about a year.
Apparently I had been spotted on the road.
I saw you in the supermarket. Tried not to look. You went back to be with Yas...you told the pigs I had parked my blue Landrover next to yours and reported me again.
You nearly ran me down on my bike turning in ahead of me the short way to your work. I volunteered to be a guinea pig at the centre while you were training in the next room. I asked your colleagues not to tell you....I saw you cycling across the bridge on the old bike on the other side.
I went in to see the Vicar of St Peter's to have a chat about us...
The church said I could go in any time. You reported me for sitting with my bike on the bend.
I am sorry the children were upset and didn't understand.
Eventually I received a 'caution'.
I hated you behaving like a perfect stranger and telling everyone our relationship was never intimate.
You told them our relationship was never a physical one.
After that night when you lay sleeping waiting for me I went to my caravan. I had finished at Grays road and didn't know what else to do. I was in limbo.
The first thing I remember is the pigs raiding it early one morning and being dragged off to prison.

When they charged me with the possession of that old firearm without a licence I
was knocked for six. It didn't even work. They charged me with a lesser offence by
mistake (Debbie G. was fit though; I nearly kissed her in the cop-shop). I rang my
mum and step-dad. Keith wanted to know what on earth I was doing with a thing
like that.
Apparently they went round and told you.
You immediately assumed I was going to kill you. What do you really take me for?
The Officers told me that I would get about eight or nine years in prison. I told my
mum that I would rather die...I thought I would die, in prison.
It was like a hell on earth. I had to live with the kind of low-life scum I have
avoided all my life.
I really didn't think I would be able to survive but my friends in Oxford supported me tremendously. They were
instrumental in getting me through it and provided the Judge with some very good references.
The police tried to paint me in the very worse light possible.

The Judge told the Prosecution that they had to stop mentioning the other things they found unless they were going to
charge me with them.
The Prosecution said that there were many more charges to come but they didn't materialize. There was a woman in the
court who kept smiling at me who seemed vaguely familiar.
A small amount of cannabis in a bag with a pipe (I had once experimented with Sarah (the manager of Headington
library), who I had gone out with briefly after you. She came in and cooked me a meal for my birthday and really
looked after me. I don't know what I would have done without her. (Unfortunately I needed a
much stronger personality).A sacrificial dagger. Some liquid I had bought on the Internet without any serious
intentions. I had money to burn in those days! What an idiot.
I received eighteen months for the time when Benji saw me closing the door.
I received two years for the firearm business.
My Solicitor's Secretary said: "What do you think of that? You will be out in March." I was greatly relieved.
Two years in prison (and I was forced to serve the full two years in prison, even
though I was released to a hostel at the half-way stage): for having a firearm I only had because I felt depressed.
It could only happen to me.
Those days in prison were the worse of my life.
I felt you thinking about me when you found my second jug, and when you found my woolly hat. The one you all
laughed at me wearing in Malta. The second jug wasn't as nice as the first one. It's face wasn't as expressive.
I could also feel your mother's sadness despite what she might have said about allowing me into the house...
Shortly before I was due out a really nasty man, who was there on some very serious charges, attacked me from behind
in a dark corridor, because he said I owed him a mars bar. It took me a while to get him down and restrain him, but by
that time he had hit me with something in my face and my blood was spurting all over the corridor and walls.
One of the officers said she had never seen so much blood.
I was in a terrible state and made a mess...
I nearly passed out.
I called the police in to press charges, and all they did was give him a 'caution.'
The Officers played tricks on me all the time. A lot of people went mad in there.
You said in one of your statements that you thought you were going mad. You are
lucky. You were mad already.
When I came out they sent me to Milton Keynes.
They told me I couldn't talk to any women without their permission because I was
so 'dangerous'.
I went to a beautician without telling them (I could have been recalled).
When I saw a woman up at the shops with the same mouth and nose as you it
made me feel very sad. A year in prison was a very long time to me.
Roger gave me some book tokens he had just received the day I was released
and took me for a curry (it was his birthday!).
Do you remember Roger? You called him an 'anorak' when you first met him, then you said he was nice.
When I came back from spending the tokens the police were waiting for me, and tried to charge me with something I had
not done.
When I eventually moved to a hostel in Norwich I was saddened to see how much time had gone by.
I was training to be a Spiritual healer at a nearby church when I met a really pretty lady in her early thirties called
Cristina. She had a first class honours in literature, and could speak four languages fluently. She had grown up in

Portugal but looked and sounded a bit Swedish. I was extremely proud of her...They were due to recall me for walking her back to her car one night and for being ten minutes late, so I went on-the-run.   I drove over to Ireland to pick up a caravan and then over to Banbury.  I got a free membership at the gym after a few months. ~Eventually I came back to Wallingford.  It all felt so surreal. I let myself in by the usual methods.

You left a postcard from your holiday in the kitchen. I did wonder why your escort had signed it G.Mills. Very formal. I don't know how I didn't wake you all slamming the door so hard.
The next time I went you were in the kitchen for ages stroking your hair on the phone. I was getting very bored, and it was bluddy cold in that garden. The spikes on the wall were no deterrent; I flew over them!
It felt so strange seeing you Elizabeth. You had hardly changed, but your hair looked a bit lighter. You were always asking Yas and people if they preferred blondes.
Benji and Emily came in and out of the room several times. I guess they were about ready for bed.
I don't know if I had been seen but Benji went to fetch your new lodger and got her to look out in the garden. He pointed but that was all. She went back upstairs. Then I saw you hide behind the door with a very
mischievous grin, peeping round it, as they all went up to bed. You scolded them up to bed.
You plonked yourself down on your computer chair with a glass of wine in one hand and a bottle in the other.
You pretended to peer round the door, and then very naughtily shoved both hands into your trousers. You made some really suggestive faces as you looked at the screen. Unfortunately I was unable to see what was on it in spite of standing in the corner with my binoculars.  You simulated sex and appeared very raunchy.
You were wearing your tweed trousers and you had your glasses on. Your middle area looked a bit loose and paunchy. Emily came to watch you and stood by your side. You nodded at the screen. She stood for a short while and then went out and shut the door...good for her! I was so sorry for you. I didn't know what to do. I have never seen anything so sad in all my life.  I could have cried. I think I did shed a few tears watching you.
Your hand went in and out all the time. Sometimes you just lolled in a stupor. You appeared to be communicating with someone and typing with great difficulty and deliberation.
After a while your glasses fell off and you slumped in your chair, with your belly extended and your shirt sticking out.
You seemed to be slurring your speech.
Then Benji came down from upstairs. He sat on the couch behind you pretending to be asleep. He kept sneaking a look out into the garden (god knows how he knew I was there) and then back at you at what you were doing. You were masturbating in front of your own children!
This went on for several minutes. He kept arching a bit closer and tried to peer over your shoulder to see what you were looking at.
You kept wafting your hand at him as if to say he had to stay put, and you couldn't help what you were doing.
I suppose he must have been about twelve by this time, although he still wasn't very tall.
Then he got up and went.
You spilt your wine.
Your trousers were split.
When you dropped your glasses you started to squint at the screen and your head tottered backwards and forwards. Then you suddenly got up and went to bed.

Am I mad to think I should have been there with you in person?
I left Emily some presents, which I know she took.
I felt uneasy the next week. As if someone were thinking about me. I thought it was the u-know-who's. I always have a sixth sense.
Driving across I felt very troubled. I even passed a panda car leaving Didcot.
I parked my car up the road and walked down. The field and woods had changed a bit....I stood on a large tree-trunk. When I got to the wall I knew something was wrong. You were all huddled together on the sofa. You looked absolutely petrified and on the edge of breaking down.  I am so sorry for that. I can never tell you how sorry.
I could not resist sending you a message as I stood in the corner on the spur of the moment. It was very foolish of me. I am very sorry for using the C-word. I meant to write hairy bush. It sounded very crude, and I never liked to be crude with you. That's when you tried to ring me. I saw you toying with a white pencil between your lips and looking for some details: probably the Eustace fellow's.
You got the children upstairs, turned the lights off, and went to lie on the back hall floor looking through the cat-flap. I hardly dared to breath. I knew if I were caught there I would be in serious trouble. I was surprised after what I had seen that you told anyone.  I knew the cops had arrived but I couldn't move until you went upstairs.

I was only just able to get away as they came around the corner with a police dog.

I cut my hand scaling a seven foot fence...Not bad for ninety odd!

I rang and said I was sorry and never meant to hurt you. Benji answered the phone. The policeman put on a funny voice pretending to be you. I could have left the area but it was cold and I didn't really know where to go.

I knew they were after me and when I was followed coming from the bike-shop the next day I knew my number was up. They dragged me from my car even though I wanted to go peacefully. I was so petrified that I actually called for my mother.

I could hardly breathe and I thought they were going to kill me. They kept calling me the most repulsive names and thumping me because of you. They told me that if I ever returned to Oxfordshire they would; "hunt me down!"

You said in your statement that you had to go to the doctor because of me and that Benji had to too. I am sorry if I added to your problems but you were seeing the doctor long before me. You made it sound as if I was the source of all your pains. You blamed me for almost everything. You said you were afraid of what I would do and that I might ruin your life...You said that you knew it was me who sent you the message because I was always sending you explicit messages, which wasn't true. You told the court that you were afraid I was going to commit a serious sexual offence against you, which as you probably knew was absolute rubbish. You told the court that you were afraid of appearing because you thought I might attack you...!

You told the court you didn't want to appear in person because you thought I might get too turned on if I heard your voice. I used to walk away from the phone your voice was so boring and monotonous sometimes.

I don't know if anyone has ever told you, but prison is not a joke, and it isn't funny.

When I received another sentence of two and half years it was a terrible shock. I received an extra year for not notifying the police of my 'change of address.....!'Eustace grinned at me when I got the sentence. A woman in the dock was almost crying.... He bragged about visiting you forty or fifty times. He said the kids came running to see him. Probably just trying to make me jealous.


I represented myself over the phone call business even though I was in such a terrible state and very out-of-sorts: no breakfast, no shower, and no sleep.

I was charged with contacting you on the phone (on my birthday)..."I'm sorry, but

I never meant to hurt you!" How is that threatening? I was referring to the broken museum fire-arm.

I was doing alright until they dredged up every horrid little detail they could from the past. They tried to make me look as bad as possible. It was very one-sided. They weren't interested that you still had some of my property, and they believed your statement that our relationship was never intimate, that you had only known me a few weeks, and that I had stalked you until you had to have psychiatric treatment and were in fear of your life.

I had to serve the remainder of the first sentence along with this new sentence, and also all the time I spent 'at-large'.

My former employers couldn't believe the severity. Neither did they think I deserved the label given me by the police and the media thanks to you.

My second sentence was even worse than the first.

I don't know how I ever got through it. It completely wore me out.

I was attacked by someone suffering from schizophrenia in the middle of the night. It just seemed to go on and on forever. When I eventually got out I was recalled for going on a library computer even though I didn't contact anyone I was told not to and had to spend another humiliating and tortuous year inside.

I was sent to HMP ******* where I went on the main wing, but had urine and even more unpleasant things thrown through my door. Some of the young men said the most revolting things to me. They threatened to slash my throat and even tried to set fire to my cell.

I couldn't help asking: what had I really done to deserve all this?

The police stopped me from going to my Writer's group and from attending my church. They warned everyone that I was dangerous before I got out, and no doubt exaggerated everything I had done. They poked their noses into everything I did. I wasn't allowed to do anything without their say so. I wasn't allowed to make any meaningful friendships.

My sister and mother were told the most spiteful and prejudiced nonsense.

Just before I came out they applied for a SOPO order, because that was the end of my sentence, and I was not on the Sex offender's register. They applied for it just so they could keep tabs on me and so they could interfere in everything I did. They told the court that I was in danger of attacking you or a member of the public and committing a serious sexual offence. They also labelled me as being a danger to children. When I stood up for myself and said that this was absolute bullshit and that we had split up because I didn't want to touch you I was accused of being aggressive.

The Magistrates peered down their snooty noses at me.

All they saw was my label and where I came from.

I totally reject this description of me.

I do apologise for not being able to tell you all this in person AND FOR MY POOR HANDWRITING...

# Fourteen year old Mastermind gets life

By Usuli Twelves | Published: October 2, 2015 | Edit

A British Judge handed down a life sentence to a young Muslim boy today for sending messages to an associate in Australia. Apparently, he had been encouraging his friend to lop his teacher's head off or shank-a-soldier in the Anzac day celebrations.

The Judge described his correspondence as "chilling," and demanded that the young man be detained until he could be "de-radicalised," whatever that means.

Calls are being made for a mandatory ten year sentence for carrying a knife.

# Womb transplants from zombies

By Peter Smith | Published: September 30, 2015 | Edit

The British Health Service is now offering womb transplants for all wombless women wanting to have children. An expensive process but worth every penny when you are trying to attract more migrants to the country.

# Matching scarf and gloves

We were in the car driving back to Norwich station when Pain-in-the-butt thanked Chris for the scarf she had knitted. By a lucky coincidence it matched her gloves.

"To change the subject. What did you mean when you said I would have to find somewhere else to live if anything happened to mum?" Silence.

"Why did you sneak up behind me and say: "I'm more successful than you will ever be!"

"I never said it! Tell him to shut-up!" she snapped.

## Word gets around By <u>Usuli Twelves</u> | Published: April 26, 2015 | <u>Edit</u>

Word certainly gets around at the Jubilee Family Centre. Gossip travels faster than grease lightning. The Elders speaking at the Sunday Service seemed to be addressing all their comments to me. Who told them is anyone's guess…

*This is the church which never hears any gossip.*

## Men get the worse By <u>Usuli Twelves</u> | Published: April 28, 2015 | <u>Edit</u>

Once again men are treated worse than women. Eight people faced the firing squad for drugs offences. Only the woman was set free.

# Pendle Witches

By <u>Usuli Twelves</u> | Published: October 14, 2015 | <u>Edit</u>

During the Pendle Witch trials Jennet Device pointed her finger at several quaking old crones, including her own mother. She accused them of flying through the air on broomsticks and partaking of union with the 'Devil,' and what is even more strange, the Jury believed her. It could never happen now.

**<u>Dear Mr Bromiley,</u>**

I was very disappointed to see you go and talk to Mrs Didwell outside our last Resident's meeting when she threatened to leave if you didn't, and then talk to Mrs Temple outside the back door. These people obviously have it in for us. Why didn't you reprimand Mrs Woodbine for kicking me, instead of saying 'excuse me,' when I had been on the path?

I understand that I am "being watched!" all the time, and that some of the Residents keep phoning the police about me. Do you know why?

NORMAN SCHWARZKOPF

*comments*

### The non-executive branch of the Little people

By Usuli Twelves | Published: April 27, 2015 | Edit

We, the non-executive branch of little folk, promise never to communicate with each other while on Google. We will never discuss ways of destabilising society, the assembling of detonators, or high explosives. Our meetings will never take place on the last Thursday of every month close to the bandstand. We will only campaign for peace and for the well-being of this wonderful human species. Our agenda will only include ways to achieve harmony and peace. We will never work as gangsters or agents of terror.

# The organ  By Usuli Twelves | Published: April 28, 2015 | Edit

Brian's mum refused to buy him an organ for eight months. She said she couldn't afford it. He said he would speak to me again if she bought him one. She did. He didn't.

### Having a grand-daughter By Usuli Twelves | Published: April 28, 2015 | Edit

Chris says she never expected to have a grand-daughter. She thought Brian was incapable. Just when you thought that was it she pipped you at the final fence Geraldine!

### Yet another black man  By Usuli Twelves | Published: April 29, 2015 | Edit

Yet another black man dies in police custody in the United States. Obama says the nation needs to do a lot of 'soul-searching'. The time for soul-searching is gone. You have to give credit where credit's due. No way this group of heroes will lie down and let the Plebs go on sticking the boot in.

### Scroungers passing  By Adumla | Published: April 29, 2015 | Edit

We are becoming a nation of lazy work shy scroungers. Why can't we just accept that losers will be losers and leave them to their play-stations?

### The bitch has been at it again By Adumla | Published: May 1, 2015 | Edit

While I was away the bitch has been in my room again. My internet activities spied on, my personal space invaded, and my weights thrown in the nearest skip. Mothers, teachers! Don't y just love em? When I came back she was on her Skype to Canada. My aunt and uncle peered from the screen as I passed.

"Why does he have to sit there?" moaned my aunty (another teacher with narrow eyes and a very suspicious face). "Doesn't he make a lot of noise when he eats!"

# Norwich County Court

By <u>Adumla</u> | Published: September 28, 2015 | <u>Edit</u>

**Bunderchook** appeared at the County Court today accused of all sorts of heinous crimes:

- banging on doors and windows

- letting down tyres

- shouting

Etc etc. An attempt was made to amend the original order:

The Prosecuting Barrister said to him:

"If you agree to the charges we can get it all over and done with today. We decided to go for an amendment instead of having you sent straight to prison!"

"Why should I go to prison," replied **Bunderchook**. "I haven't done anything wrong and these idiots are nothing but liars!"

Comments

## Factually incorrect: more stories from the Jubilee family Centre

By <u>Adumla</u> | Published: September 28, 2015 | <u>Edit</u>

Come on. Admit it Simon. All this punishment for sins and divine retribution rubbish is exactly that. What kind of God would send his son to earth to be humiliated and tortured to death? How bizarre to think that someone could take away another person's 'sins.'
We came to talk to you about the bullying and lying we were experiencing earlier this year from a certain group of nasty neighbours but all you wanted to talk about was *'no sex before marriage please.'*
We hadn't done anything wrong yet we were still getting picked on and tales were coming from Bure Valley Zoo right up to the Jubilee Centre which were factually incorrect.
*Why did you have to grab hold of my handlebars?*
As the Director and Church leader I would have thought you might at least admit that you received my post?

THE REPLY->
Today at 5:03 PM

Hi there!  The teaching of the Bible couldn't be clearer – sin is serious and has eternal consequences, but God in his infinite mercy and justice has made the way for our sin to be dealt with, and for us to be made right with Him, through Jesus' death and resurrection. If this wasn't the purpose of Jesus' death then it was nothing more than a terrible accident or tragedy.  What kind of God would send His Son to die a horrible death in our place? One who loves us far more than we could ever deserve.  This is the cornerstone of what it means to believe in Jesus and be a Christian.  I would be really happy to look through the Bible with you to see what God has to say about all this. Please let me know if you'd like to do this?

As I have said many times before, we have never heard any rumours about Christine and yourself from the Bure Valley Zoo (or any other source) – we have only heard what you have told us. This we have listened to carefully and prayed with you and tried to give you considered counsel. The matter of the physical nature of your relationship together is something that we needed to discuss with you as Christine is a member of long-standing in the church and therefore we have a pastoral responsibility for her welfare (physical, emotional and spiritual) which we want to uphold with love and grace (to the both of you).

You are welcome to attend ACC but if you have matters of disagreement with us over our teaching you need to either: (a) come and discuss this with the leadership in a mature manner, or (b) think seriously about whether you would be more comfortable worshipping somewhere else. What is not acceptable is making barbed comments – to me or anyone else – whose only purpose is to put down the other person (and their beliefs). Please do not do this again OR I WILL MAKE SURE YOU REGRET IT!

As I have said I would be really pleased to meet up with you and discuss these things properly.
"Love your neighbour as thyself!"

*Simon Bullshiter*

# The End

By Surloin Steak | Published: November 27, 2014 | Edit

It's finally the end of 'Plebgate.'  If the Judge says he called them it then he did.
British Justice has triumphed once again.  Andrew Mitchell will be forced to pay £3,000,000 in damages. Take your bike out the *right way* next time lovey. I suppose this is the moment to roll out that well *trumped up* phrase: "paying for what he's done."
The Judge declared that PC Toby Rowland 'did not have the 'imagination' to fabricate such a descriptive term.'  Why not, plenty of them do?
What are you trying to say, Justice Mitting?
Oh, I get it!  "Thick!" In other words. It's official then.
Who's going to take any notice of a tart of a Judge anyway?
"FUCKING PLEBS!"
Comments 1 comments

# Fritzl's cellar

By Surloin Steak | Published: November 27, 2014 | Edit

The cellar of Josef Fritzl was something of a love-nest. After all, he did father seven or eight more children down there. It can't have been torture all of the time. When I read that he'd been labelled a 'pervert' I was fuming. Surely, if you want to look at real perversions then homosexuality and lesbianism must figure quite high up the list. At first his daughter tried to protect him, but it was only when she was going to be charged herself that she decided to turn nasty. If they had been the last couple left on earth, and the fate of the human species had lain in their hands, then there would have been no recriminations or moral outrage. Poor old Josef Fritzl. He'll be in a wheelchair when he gets out. Wouldn't it be funny if one of his illegitimate offspring went on to become a brilliant scientist who invented a cure for hogwash?

## Batsman slain by hurling missile

By Surloin Steak | Published: November 27, 2014 | Edit

All this could have been avoided if he had not deliberately turned his head and a leather ball had not been hurled towards him with the sole intention of getting him out. I have not yet heard if they intend to charge anyone with murder.

Comments

# Duty

By Lawrence van Der Splurgen | Published: November 26, 2014 | Edit

It is the duty of every free thinking person to view with suspicion every story published in print. To question every statement made. To call into question versions of the truth which are one sided, inaccurate and concocted by Authority.

STREET BINS.

# Spastics

By Lawrence van Der Splurgen | Published: November 26, 2014 | Edit

It has long been my opinion that we should put severely disabled people to death at birth. To gently ease them out of a troubled and unproductive existence. But who would have the balls to say so?

# Jihadists to face Justice

By Lawrence van Der Splurgen | Published: November 26, 2014 | Edit

How can anyone believe in this shit? To face 'justice?'

As if so called 'British' justice were better than anywhere else.

The powers that be have already had to backtrack on their *draconian* measures to jail anyone who has had the decency to fight for their beliefs: who want to help the injured, who want to learn how to fire a weapon or handle high explosives.

The police force run training camps all the time and no-one throws them into prison, even if they shoot an innocent commuter to death during target practise.

## Shoot the Pope

By Sarin | Published: November 25, 2014 | Edit

The Pope has made a plea to the European Community to open its gates to more migrants from the African continent before the Mediterranean becomes a coffin. Nice to know the Pope is so in touch with public opinion.

Well, what do you expect from a 'Catholic?'

Mr Farage commented: "he was just drawing attention to how outdated and inept the Community really is…" Nice one Nigel!

## COMMENTS?

# Race riots

By Surloin Steak | Published: November 25, 2014 | Edit

Well come on.  What happens in the US usually happens here a few weeks later.

# No such thing as innocent

By Surloin Steak | Published: November 25, 2014 | Edit

When people are found guilty of something they didn't do it doesn't really matter, because they must have been 'guilty' of *something*…

# The murder of Lee Rigby

By Surloin Steak | Published: November 25, 2014 | Edit

The murder of Lee Rigby could not have been prevented by giving the State yet more powers of scrutiny and surveillance over the internet.  If it hadn't been him, it would have been someone else.  If they hadn't communicated via the internet it would have been by another method.  What really needs to be understood are the reasons British soldiers are being attacked in the first place. *Aren't they killing people abroad all the time?*

Comments

# Voyeurism

By <u>Surloin Steak</u> | Published: November 25, 2014 | <u>Edit</u>

It is now against the law to look at people and especially to take their photos. That's why the State does it all the time. You could be sent to prison, have your home searched, and end up with a very sinister reputation.

"Here's look'n at ya kid."

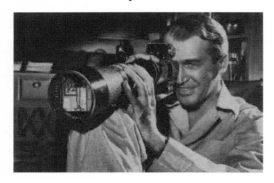

# Yet more surveillance

By <u>Lawrence van Der Splurgen</u> | Published: November 23, 2014 | <u>Edit</u>

Theresa May has just announced the intention to give yet more powers of surveillance and invigilation to the police. This is the same organisation which was found to be shifty and dishonest, after attempting to get a member of her own party dismissed from his job as a democratically elected MP.
The intention is to keep a track on any criminal activity and to cover any gaps in national security. In other words: to pry into every e-mail, text message, or envelope they like. When is it going to stop?

# Tree of life

By <u>Surloin Steak</u> | Published: November 22, 2014 | <u>Edit</u>

**World leaders live in dread**

By <u>Rumpelstiltskin</u> | Published: March 30, 2015 | <u>Edit</u>

Following an e-mail blunder the dates of birth of many of the World's leaders were sent to the wrong incipient. Even though the information was destroyed it was all somehow leaked to the press. Makes you wonder!

# Italian legal system favours the guilty

By <u>Rumplestiltskin</u> | Published: March 30, 2015 | <u>Edit</u>

Amanda Knox and Raffa Sollecito can expect many millions of dollars in compensation after sticking to their tale that they didn't commit any offence. If you come from a wealthy and influential family you are far better pleading innocent.
No wonder they are smiling.  Nice hair by the way.

# No sexist images for toddlers

By <u>Surloin Steak</u> | Published: November 22, 2014 | <u>Edit</u>

Tesco's have decided to remove newspapers containing obscene images of women from ground level.  This is in case any sweet and innocent child stumbling along with their hand on the shopping trolley were to see a breast or two.  It could totally warp their minds.

# Patronising images

By <u>Rumpelstiltskin</u> | Published: November 21, 2014 | <u>Edit</u>

That does it!  I'm going to send as many as I can.

# Cons lose to Reckless

By <u>Rumpelstiltskin</u> | Published: November 21, 2014 | <u>Edit</u>

The Tories threw everything they could into yesterday's bi-election and still came off second best.  The non-liberal candidate didn't even get 1% of the vote.  That's what you get when you join the Conservatives.

# THE TEN COMMANDMENTS

By Rumpelstiltskin | Published: November 21, 2014 | Edit

Do not trust anyone who says they have heard the word of 'God'

Do not be cowered by threats from a supposed omnipotent being

Take pride in the archetypal principles

Give vent to your anger

Do anything you like on a Sunday

Treat your parents with respect if they do the same to you

Kill only in the name of Allah or pork scratchings

Sleep with whoever is good for you

Take from the rich but don't give it to the poor

Remain true to your friends

Disobey every rule in the book

# McCann abducted by aliens

By Adumla | Published: March 29, 2015 | Edit

I have my own theory about what happened to little Madeleine McCann. I think she was abducted by aliens, eager to learn more about what makes us all tick. I know there were some strange lights seen in the sky over *Praia da Luz* that awful night.

Either that or she was shoved in a sack and taken away in a hurry by a rapacious sex-fiend.

## Last night's pork crackling

By Godfrey Winklebacker | Published: March 29, 2015 | Edit

We were standing in the queue ready for second helpings when Simon spoke on the loudspeaker. A teacher standing behind us in the queue had already been up and told him.

Comments

# Jail for watching videos

By Godfrey Winklebacker | Published: March 29, 2015 | Edit

A lot of the most famous films watched by adults contain images of violence, yet the nanny state is about to give the police permission to arrest parents for allowing their children to watch violent videos.
*When I worked as a Private Investigator I was invited to watch some of the most graphic kiddie porn down at the local nick in their own cinema room (I rejected the offer).

Isn't this new law going to give the State yet more powers of surveillance and intrusion. What's it going to feel like with two police officers sitting at your table all night?

A headteacher said that watching videos at an early age *sexualises* youngsters (trust an interfering schoolteacher). She complained of a 'lack of empathy' between parents and children. She said that watching these sorts of videos was 'damaging' and wanted to know what could be done about it. Once again we heard the words 'safe-guarding,' and *for your protection.*
I don't know if you've bothered to look Mrs, but adolescent teenagers are full of hormones, and will be experimenting with sex without any kind of encouragement. A fact of life! Live with it. Of course, sex is a very terrible thing, except if you're a teacher.

I've a good mind to report one of you to Social Services.

## Isolation of criminals

By Godfrey Winklebacker | Published: March 29, 2015 | Edit

If you have ever been in trouble it is nearly impossible to get car insurance, a job, or a secure place to live. This makes it more certain that you will end up back in trouble, to the delight of society and the police.

# Andy Crick's girlfriend

By Peter Smith | Published: March 28, 2015 | Edit

He doesn't have one.

# Cameron says...

By <u>Adumla</u> | Published: March 28, 2015 | <u>Edit</u>

Cameron says that the Labour party are a load of incompetent sneering Socialist gits.

He said nothing about the rest of the House of Commons being a pack of greedy self indulgent twats.

Pretty much like the rest of society then…

# Spanish Inquisition alive and kicking

By <u>Peter Smith</u> | Published: March 27, 2015 | <u>Edit</u>

If you were ever worried we were becoming a more 'tolerant' society think again.   The Spanish Inquisition is still alive and kicking in your living room.

- burning at the stake

- special terms for heretics and repeat offenders

- strangulation offered for a quick confession

- full public support

- punished even after you are dead

- cuts out the cancer in your soul forever

- once behind bars we'll do what we like with you

***Unable to poison others with your thinking!***

For questioning the facts and impeding the work of the Inquisition you may be hung drawn and quartered and your body fed to the vultures. Why wait for that knock at the door in the dead of night.  Hand yourself in straight away as an 'act of faith'. Hand us your genitals and you'll never see pleasure again!

\* Reliant upon snitches everywhere

# Don't upset the driver

By Peter Smith | Published: March 26, 2015 | Edit

Don't upset the cabin staff:

1 Scare the passengers half to death with a sudden nose dive
2 Set mad gunman loose
3 Start screaming "we're going to crash!" over the intercom
4 Lock the pilot out of the cockpit
5 Lose right wing or left tailboard engine

Shake a six:

Plough straight into mountainside or multi-storey building

# Police persecution of celebrities

By Rumpelstiltskin | Published: March 26, 2015 | Edit

In the nineteen sixties and seventies the police were involved in a long running vendetta against the rich and famous: people whose creative freedom and lifestyle made them slightly envious.  Their main obsession was with drugs.  Obviously drugs are very wicked, and it was the responsibility of the Plods to eradicate this serious menace to decent society.   Certain officers made it their crusade to 'clean up' society and make these *rogues* do as they were bloody well told.  Of course, they were supported by the Government of the day and their lackeys in the legal *industry*.  One of their principal targets were ***the Rolling Stones.***  It was their determination to get one of the Stones in prison by which time they could run around telling everyone what evil felons they were. *In one dawn raid they actually found someone smoking a joint and having sex with his girlfriend.*  Though not at the same time.

Apart from getting the Rolling Stones fined for exposure after they all went out for a pee the Met were unable to get either Keith Richards or Mick Jagger behind bars for more than a few hours.  Finally one of the mob received five years for perjury, so it was in fact one of the *officers* who ended up totally screwed (*the end justifies the means?*).

I suppose that's what happens when you give brain dead semi-morons the power of arrest.

## COMMENTS

# Victoria hated sex

By <u>Rumpelstiltskin</u> | Published: March 25, 2015 | <u>Edit</u>

The Victorian age in England was known as a puritanical time of sedate religious austerity? Scottish gamekeepers aside THE HEAD OF STATE was totally peed off by the death of her husband, Prince Albert. The era was largely influenced by the attitude of the queen herself who ruled for sixty four years and had a very prudish view of sex.

By the time she died in 1901 she already had one hundred and ninety descendants, having given birth to nine children.

# Clarkson "crossed the line"

By <u>Rumpelstiltskin</u> | Published: March 25, 2015 | <u>Edit</u>

At last we have a result. Jeremy Clarkson has been fired from 'Top Gear' after what a BBC exec called "sustained physical and verbal abuse!" Could be human after all.

The more people who stand up to authority and political correctness the better.

# Greedy Doctors

By <u>Sarin</u> | Published: March 24, 2015 | <u>Edit</u>

Lokum doctors are ripping the health service off with bills of thousands of pounds a day. Poor doctors! Over-stretched, underpaid, and prone to handing over confidential information at the drop of a hat.

## Stewart witch-hazel

By Sarin | Published: March 24, 2015 | Edit

Stewart gave me a strong piece of wood today. He said it came from the ancient oak forests of Ireland. He makes catapults at £30 each but I'm not sure if they would be powerful enough to do what I had in mind. Poor Stewart has a hearing impediment, but it hasn't prevented him from listening to Fat-Arse.

## Sleep deprivation

By Sarin | Published: March 24, 2015 | Edit

An hour's deep sleep packed with wild dreams and whims leaves you refreshed and completely calm. The room needs to be dark and warm with a source of ventilation. A fan helps to drown out distracting intrusions and beats a soft and regular rhythm. A hot shower and a nice hard shag also help you relax. Without good sleep madness can develop.

# Another Afro-American execution

By Adumla | Published: April 9, 2015 | Edit

Yet another black male has been cut down by a white American policeman after being stopped for a minor traffic violation. Eight bullets. For what? The police continue to lie and cover up their mistakes. This is just the tip of the ice-berg.

Mind you. The Politicians are just as slippery.

comments

# Chinese women arrested for arguing

By Godfrey Winklebacker | Published: March 29, 2015 | Edit

Five young activists have been arrested and put in prison by the Authorities in China after trying to highlight the rights of women. The Chinese Authorities have told the West to mind its own business (a euphemism for 'fk off!'), and that it is perfectly within the law for them to throw the women into jail for 'causing a quarrel.' One of the poor women has suffered a heart-attack after hours of intense interrogation.

Isn't it always the case that Governments will introduce new laws or twist old ones to suppress the voice of the critic when ever they feel threatened and that nothing will ever be done to resist their *received authority* until people stand up in open rebellion.

It's never been about right and wrong, it's only ever been about power. The power to control, the power to tell people what to do, to make Commandments and conquests.

# Muslim backlash

By Lawrence van Der Splurgen | Published: November 20, 2014 | Edit

If I was a young Muslim required to go and fight Assad I would jump at the chance. I thought the British Government were ready to attack him themselves not that long ago!

There will be a civil war in this country before long and no amount of special banning orders will suffice. Any current banning orders will have to continue indefinitely.

It really needs a strong General to organise them into battalions with strict codes of conduct.

Comments

# School Photographer jailed for taking pictures

By <u>Bird Dung</u> | Published: August 27, 2015 | <u>Edit</u>

When I met with Peabody today he was even more excited than usual.

A catalogue of photographs had been passed around the station, with the Director and one or two of the Senior Officers having first sniff.

By the time the albums reached him they were already torn, with several of the photographs missing or photocopied.

A Senior Detective said that the Photographer had committed **a serious breach of "trust"** in taking the photographs, but she was extremely impressed by the lengths to which he had gone: many of the photographs were taken from very awkward and revealing angles.

Surely, losing his job should be punishment enough?  Not as if he was a drunken motorist or a binman with a history of heart failure.

"That'll be the more tolerant society we are always hearing about!"

"It's a big world."

And not enough perversions to go round in it.

# NO ESCAPE FROM 'JUSTICE'

By Lawrence van Der Splurgen | Published: December 19, 2014 | Edit

Plans are underway to punish any crime, however long ago in history.

The beneficiaries of that crime will have all their proceeds confiscated by the Treasury.

## British Army cleared of blame

By Surloin Steak | Published: December 17, 2014 | Edit

The British Army were cleared of torture in Iraq today. Thank goodness it was an old toady from the British Establishment leading the enquiry. The less serious charges of starvation, binding, and castration were upheld. I will not have these poor murderers pestered.

# Definitely no room for geriatrics

By Rumpelstiltskin | Published: December 20, 2014 | Edit

What is this crazy Western obsession for keeping everything alive well past its sell-by date. What is it all about?

If food is off, or going off, then you throw it away.

There is no glory in old age or the deterioration of the body.

Better to die young in battle than to live to be 'old.'

## Chinks

By Surloin Steak | Published: December 19, 2014 | Edit

Chinks have appeared in the armour of UKIP leader Nigel Farage. His poll rating has dived today, but is still higher than the current Prime Minister David Cameron. What he really needs are high calibre candidates who are willing to put their name and reputation on the line. Mr Farage refused to waterboard one of his members for using *quite ordinary and uncomplex language* just because a few media tykes said he should.

Comments

# Soup kitchens for the poor

By Usuli Twelves | Published: December 21, 2014 | Edit

During the nineteen twenties a young assassin rose to power in New York who went on to become the archetypal gangster.

There were three versions of the truth in those days:

• *Traditional Government (State sponsored terrorism in which only those laws issued by the State were accepted as being just and in which armies could murder at will)*

• *Capone Industries truth (the law of the jungle)*

• *Catholic church dogma:*

*(in the middle ages people could be burnt at the stake for disagreeing with their views, or if you believed in another form of Christianity you could be put to death as a 'heretic')*

Each gang had its own strict code of ethics and ways of law enforcement.

Each gang could be cold, vindictive and cruel.

The only difference between the Gangs is that the Al Capone Gang didn't believe in remorse and any punishment they exacted finished after you were dead.  Al Capone was also the first person to institute soup kitchens for the poor, which shows that in his case you shouldn't really judge a book by its cover.

# The Ballad of little Robin BY LANDRU (1923)

*'I am that little Robin, will you not give me your bread?'*

This is the story of Little Robin, who lived long ago before men had entered the forest, when the earth was still young and beautiful.

When pure white streams became thin blue rivers and the air was still fresh on the way from the sea.

It all began one dim and desolate night when the freezing breeze howled among the tree-tops and two dark specks darted like pin-drops in the scud of the gale. When they eventually settled on a beam of the Oak they entwined their final twig and leaf to the nest.

Before long three fine eggs lay on the pillow of their refuge and Mother Robin warmed them with the fullness of her heart.

She listened to the purling of the flow.

A terrible storm descended on the woodland that night. Full-grown trees were uprooted from their beds and fear swept the saplings on the floor of the forest. A haze of seed showered down from the Elm.

The deer and the antelope raced for shelter along with the red squirrels.

The hare and the badger scampered to their burrows as two enormous Terrorhawks rampaged among the turmoil.

From high in the sky they caught sight of the hatchery where Mother Robin sat on her eggs. Father Robin charged fearlessly up to meet them as they dive-bombed from the fog of darkness.

His cries could be heard above the wind but no-one but the Moon rallied to his cause. Just as the first cracks appeared on a shell Father Robin was snuffed-out by a lunge from their beaks.

He cried out to the Lord of the forest but still perished in an instant.

Mother Robin was dragged from her nest and carried off to a nearby lake.

The three eggs were turfed out of their nest by the Hawks.

Just as he was falling through the air Little Robin drew his first breath and let out a shrill little cry.

His head scraped against the bark of the tree as he fell and three little drops of blood splashed on the grass as he tumbled towards the earth.

He quickly lost consciousness when he hit the ground and his tiny leg was broken. Though the moss of the ground broke his fall little Robin lay in a heap on the floor...

When he awoke he saw the Owl staring down at him from the surrounding greenery. His head had been wrapped in a white bandage and his foster parents cradled him in their arms. They sang sweet melodies.

He felt his eyes slowly closing...

The Owl said that everything in the forest had a Guardian spirit, from the stones in the brooke, to the sycamore tree and its leafs.

From beyond the mist a beam of light fell through the branches and the Sun fluttered its lashes again.

The Nightingales were a very well to do family in the area.

Robin was their only son.

They did everything they could to make him happy and to teach him how to behave impeccably in the world.

Under the guidance of the wise old Owl he learnt that not all the tallest trees bore the sweetest fruit.

The schoolhouse was built in the branches of a writhen Oak.

No feathers ever grew again on his wounds.

He never became one of the flock.


The cuckoo said that Little Robins were only allowed to eat droppings from the trees and that he had probably never even had a real father.

"He could lie in a nutshell," sniffed the smart swallow.

"He could certainly do with a worm," frowned the goose.

"Little Robin will stay small forever!" nodded the fieldmouse.

But when Little Robin sang the sun arose on the sea.

His singing soared into paradise.

Before the spring gave way to summer and the bright poppies brimmed the open meadows he grew his adult plumage.

On the journey to school he lay his red berries on the graves of his sisters.

He sang like a beam on a summer's day.

He sang at the waterfall, and the rivers of life suddenly sprang from the rocks.

The spirits of his sisters rose up and floated into the trees. He saw them wave and fly away.

He sang to the squirrel and the squirrel chirped with him.

He asked if there was any sign from the lake···

He spoke to the mistletoe, the rainbow and the rain. He sang to the flowers about the May-flies and the stars.

"Here is a wisp of straw to help keep your family warm my cousin sparrow."

His reflection rippled in the pool.

"My dear apple-tree. Your branches are filled with so many heavy fruits."

From the cornfield he robbed the rich to feed the poor.

At the brooke he sang where the *prime feather* glowed and the honeysuckle smelled sweet.

He carolled where the grass had been moistened by the morning's fingers.

One day however, he passed the garden of his one true love.

She had a voice like no-one else in the world.

She warbled as she hung out her washing.

Little Robin hid in the hedgerow and couldn't utter a sound.

He wanted desperately to meet the owner of this beautiful voice but he was much too shy for formal introductions.

He found an empty horse-chestnut shell and tied it to his head.

When Gwendoline sang he answered with some notes of his own.

They were the most beautiful sounds that had ever sprung from the breath of a robin.

When Gwendoline heard them she could only gasp and catch her tears in the apron.

Little Robin rolled his tomato to her gate.

He raced the sunbeams as they came down from heaven and chased the dew-drops from the top of the rose-petals.

"Gwendoline Gwendoline will you please be my bride be my bride?"

A gentle wind played among the branches.

One day she even caught a glimpse of him...

Gwendoline bird stood at the door with her mother.

"A robin who sings like a nightingale?"

No-one would believe her, least of all the cuckoo.

Rumours circulated around the village that a little robin had been *stealing* corn from the cornfield.

Then the magpie said that all the stardust had vanished from the morning meadow.

Grass-snake said he had even stolen tunes from the Nightingales.

The Wren said he was not even worth considering.

Gwendoline's mother said that he would certainly come to nothing.

Little Robin summoned up all his courage.

He hobbled towards them with his stick.

Gwendoline's mother shielded her daughter with her wing.

To Robin's horror they threw acorns at him and chased him down the hill.

He tottered limping over the wall.

The wise old Owl was exceedingly sorry to see his distress.

"Why so sad and downcast my little Robin?  In this life we are
fated to lose that which we hold most dear. At night the Sun dies, and
travels through the Underword...let us take a look in my tea-pot and I will

tell you all you need to know!"

"The wind will teach you how to fly every inch a king, for the wood is deeper than the well.  Here, my Little Robin, is an *innocent wish*."

"There is a kind of stream which can  blow life into one and a new dawn will rise before you."

"I have a very special mission for you."

"Very soon there will be no more berries on the trees and the leaves will all have fallen."

"The lark will no longer sing in the lower meadow and flowers will no longer bloom along the shores of the river."

"The roof above us all is paling and the dreadful dark is coming on."

"Go in search of the king of the forest and ask for his help."

"How will I know where to find him?" asked Little Robin.

"Simply follow your heart!" smiled the Owl.  He winked and cocked his head to one side.

"Courage in your heart of Oak and be fearless to your grave!"


When the new day dawned Robin flew with bigger and bigger branches.  After many Moons he could lift the fallen trunk of the Elm.

He could spin so fast that the twigs around him formed a whirlwind.

Little Robin became stronger than a hurricane.

He flew away from the forest.

Below him it appeared like a small oasis in a sea of sand.

A swirl of sycamore twirled to the ground.

Round his neck hung a little bag.

He flew over other forests.

He flew over houses where the smoke drifted up to meet him and tiny children pointed into the sky.

Past half-clad men who beat with their hammers and sparks flew all around.

A flock of starlings heading south...

"I am searching for the King of the Wide-wood," he called.

"Search for him on *higher* ground!" bellowed their leader as they turned.

He flew over seas and rivers, over many kingdoms.

As the winds grew more solemn from the top of each evergreen he wove together a coat of emerald.

He pinned his cloak together with a sprig of mistletoe.

He flew through many ages, along many pathways.

Fishes lifted their heads from the stream as he darted by.

He flapped over temples and strange cities where a different chanting was heard. He glided through the fog on a cool current until he rested at last on a hard piece of rock.

Little Robin began to sing as the flakes of snow fell from the grey sky. He chased a snowdrop over the tip of a spear.

A finger raised itself towards the heavens.

A shooting star fell from the vault.

Snow crumbled beneath the soldier's feet.

Suddenly he heard a voice crying out, as if from a wilderness.

It cried: "Father, father, why hast though forsaken me?"

"For many hours have I suffered on this timber."

His body shivered like tinsel in a winter gale as a lightning flash lit up the whole scene. Streams of red ran down the man's forehead and into his eyes.

Little Robin flew over to the man and hovered in front of him.

The land seemed to shudder and the whole world begin to groan.

His eyes suddenly fluttered open at the sound of his beating wings.

They were both white and colourless.

"I am searching for the king-of-the-forest!" chirped Little Robin.

A great crown of thorns roosted on the top of his head.

Vicious spikes were sticking into his flesh.

A green shawl of ivy hung over his shoulder. The hair of his mane was matted in blood.

Little Robin dodged between the blades which were stabbed up at him.

He flew round the bar and landed on the cross-beam.

It was there that he lay his 'forget-me-not.'

"I have brought you all the herbs of the forest, one mistletoe leaf and the sweet smell of honeysuckle."

"I bring you a pure and refreshing fragrance."

The flowers he held glittered like a flame in the heart of the Sun.

"If you rub this garland on your brow it is said that it will cure all the worries of a troubled heart."

He gave the man a shell of rose-water from the rivers of his birth.

As the man began to drink a sudden burst of colour electrified his eyes.

"What shall we now, my Little Robin?" he said.

"To bring joy to the land I have been born into this heartless sorrow. My hands have been pierced by cruel nails until my wood cried out."

"Are not my orchards plentiful. Do my cedars still stand proud on the edge of the mount. Are all my creatures warm and safe. Is there enough food in their larder? Are my lakes still a haven of white, my valleys lush with palm?"

"Are the roses of my garden still able to bloom?"

Little Robin hung in the air and removed each of the thorns in turn.

A single tear ran down the bridge of his nose.

As it dropped through the air it turned into a tiny gem.

It began to drizzle slowly at first and then it became a raging downpour.

As Robin looked into the man's eyes he could see all his friends back home: Gwendoline hanging out her washing, the hills and rivers, the Nightingales out shopping. As he peered ever deeper he even saw his own mother.

"Little Robin, my Little Robin," she carolled. "When will you be returning home for supper?"

"Were you caught stealing corn from the cornfield?" he asked the Man.

The man began to laugh and the greenery around him shake as he filled his lungs.  The wood seemed to moan and the mist around them grow more scarlet.  He let-out a tremendous stream of sound which changed into a loud roar.  The birds in the reeling sky started to quiver as the lord-of-beasts sank his head and the snow began to melt.

A silver ring appeared on Robin's shin.

The air became thick with a shower of pale pink anemones.

"It is just as if my mother kissed me!" he warbled.

His proud little breast brushed against the man's skin and soaked up some drops of his blood.

His ruff became strengthened and his head became healed.  He no longer noticed the pain.

Little Robin sang in sadness.  He remembered his promise to the forest.

He flew between swords and the words of angry men.

He flew over rivers and strange houses and all the way round the world.

He flew to the Sun and the Moon and beyond the stars high up in the sky.

He flew over woods and unknown forests.

Little Robin flew faster than a bolt of lightening down a branch.

He flew over seas and mountains until he could feel a breath of sunshine again on his cheeks.  In his beak he carried 'a single blossoming shoot.'

A snowy radiance sprang from twig to twig.

He threw apples to children in the streets below who caught them thankfully in their arms. A great storm was brewing in the forest that night.

All the animals had to run for shelter and the birds called out in alarm.

A thunderbolt had blown down the school house.

Many seeds had been lost and a lot of salmon had been found dead at the side of the river.  The badger had seen hunters armed with bow and arrows on the fringe of the heartwood.

As the darkness grew a fire was burning in the the orchard which lit up the whole place.  It was even rumoured that a bleak Sheriff had entered the wood and had begun cutting down groves. Some of the little creatures had been caught in a net while some of the larger animals had been rounded up. The living roots had been sapped of all their essence. Hardly a blade of grass was to be seen. Some of the little creatures feared that the Sun had died and that flowers would never bloom again in spring.

Except in the tree house, where a lantern swung beside a reddish flame.

Two enormous Terror-hawks dived across the forest ahead of Little Robin. An ear-piercing shriek howled from their bill as they pursued their quarry among the underwood. One of them had the cuckoo in his beak. The other raided Mrs Robin's garden for Gwendoline.

All the forest froze as Little Robin charged to the rescue.

He chased the hawks ferociously across the plain and into the sky.

A terrible battle ensued in which Robin lost the use of an eye.

One of them escaped but crashed into a cliff in the distance.

Little Robin dashed the other by his huge talon against the Oak, where he fell dead. The other creatures chased the invaders from the land as a bright ball of colour followed their path.

Little Robin lay in the arms of those he loved.

A large red patch lay on his coat where his heart must have been.

It was said that one touch of his heart could bring the whole forest back to life again. All the guardians of the forest were dressed in green as they stood beside him at the Tapas-tree. On the roots of the woodland they prayed.

"It was a long time ago, but some things will always be remembered," cooed the Owl. Little Robin attempted to sing.

He sang about a time when the earth was still young and beautiful before mankind had even entered the desert.

When pure white streams became pale blue rivers and the air was still fresh on the way to the sea. When golden roots could speak and dryads walked down the banks of the Sun to bathe.

"I am that Little Robin. Will you not give me your bread?"

# Has anyone seen Kevin?

By Rumpelstiltskin | Published: December 7, 2014 | Edit

Has anyone seen 'Kevin' the bodybuilder?  I split my sides when he came on
and posed beside the remaining contestants of 'Man o Man.'

He seems to have completely vanished from the records.

Perhaps Chris Tarrant will know?

# Politicians with permanent smirks

By Adumla | Published: March 31, 2015 | Edit

Well, I can name Ed Balls and Tony Teflon for two.   I would have said Michael Portillo, but
his is more of a scowl.  Theresa May seems to have a cross between a smirk and a grin.  It's
all that power I think.

"See the shirt on that!"

# Eleanor de Freitas

By <u>Surloin Steak</u> | Published: December 17, 2014 | <u>Edit</u>

It certainly looks as if Eleanor De Freitas went out shopping for sex aids with her alleged attacker just a short time after. There have been a lot of cases like this. Stick that in your festering horse-bucket Andrea Dworkin. From the video footage she looks unhurried, happy, and raring to go. In a country where you can now be charged with rape just for touching someone in the genital area I wouldn't be surprised if he got a life sentence.

It's only a crime if the cross-dresser in the ridiculous horse-hair wig says it is.

I have my own theory about why she turned him in: he forgot the batteries.

# Angelina Jolie

By <u>Sarin</u> | Published: December 13, 2014 | <u>Edit</u>

So, you're married to a famous movie star.

You get paid millions every year.

Someone doesn't like the *grinning doll* look.

They think you've got 'big ears.'

A Sony Executive sent an **'unflattering' e-mail.**

Grow up. For fk's sake!

# Race riots in the US

By <u>Sarin</u> | Published: December 13, 2014 | <u>Edit</u>

Protesters are filling the Streets of New York and all around the country to protest at the way young unarmed black men are being killed by the police. Black lives do matter. Once you start to notice how nasty and belligerent the police are towards young black men it begs the question:

HOW MANY OTHER GROUPS OF PEOPLE ARE MURDERED BY THE POLICE?

Surely, it's only a matter of time before there are more riots against the police in the United Kingdom following the increase in State intrusion, and a whole draft of new laws against the Muslim population and others.

The police *lying racist bullies…*

Surely not.

# The Bill Cosby witchhunt

By <u>Sarin</u> | Published: December 6, 2014 | <u>Edit</u>

## The Newspapers

By <u>Sarin</u> | Published: December 6, 2014 | <u>Edit</u>

Today we will pretend to despise everything sexual. We will get up on our soap box and preach to the wicked and superficial.

Tomorrow it will be different.

## You'd think Labour would be better

By <u>Rumpelstiltskin</u> | Published: December 2, 2014 | <u>Edit</u>

You would think that when the Labour party got into office they would do what they promised and reduce inequality, narrow the gap between rich and poor, and have a fairer selection process. All female short lists are not a fair selection process.

Quite the opposite. They build more prisons, suck up to their friends in high places, and make every effort they can to introduce yet more laws to persecute, control and subjugate the people.

# End of the National Health Service

By Surloin Steak | Published: December 11, 2014 | Edit

Why are doctors prescribing billions of pounds worth of drugs to patients who don't really need them?  What has that got to do with patient welfare?

Some patients are just too lazy and petulant to do anything at all about their weight.  No wonder there's a rise in diabetes.

When I worked in the Health Service all they seemed to care about was money.  I was proud of the work I did.  I cared about the people I looked after.

"My husband likes me just the way I am!"

Comments

# The new South Basildon candidate

By Lawrence van Der Splurgen | Published: December 10, 2014 | Edit

Thank you for that Jeff.

I will try to get along to a meeting but it's dependent upon a list of factors.

Perhaps I can help in other ways?

**Concerning the choice of Neil Hamilton as your new candidate:**

Whereas I think he is a very charming, quite likeable and articulate gentleman who has probably had a less than favourable press I think he comes to you with a tarnished reputation.  It's right to have 'big' names joining the party, but there may be more negatives than positives in this case.

It may be that given more time people will come to recognise him as an honest and upright person, but he tends to come across as quite a distant secretive individual. The public perception would be one of mistrust. As an ex-Tory he is probably used to sponging off the weaker members of society and he has *already had problems* with expenses.  I believe the party was quite correct to highlight the donations given by hard up pensioners. For this to work he would need a lot more time in the spotlight to put across the better part of his personality and his dormant sincerity.  I suspect Christine Hamilton would have been a better selection choice.

# Demise of Michael Moore (hamburger man)

By Rumpelstiltskin | Published: December 7, 2014 | Edit

Does anyone know what has become of Michael Moore?
I heard he collapsed into a mound of fat and pus.

the entrance of the Wasteland in the calm of the bereaved storm.

A rustle of twigs sizzled where the hungry *Beast* stood shivering below the mantle of silver birch. He had certainly built-up a head of steam.

On the strait patch of ground which trickled from the surrounding scud a creature miraculously appeared and stamped its hoof impatiently for the sodden mound of turf.

The *Flash* tottered in amazement, magically transported by the wavering spell of 'liberty',..he smiled and tried to neutralize the migrant with the soft concord of truce.

In the cool mist of midnight, wrapped by the overhanging sprigs of spinney, the inner sense of the *Thunderbuck Ram* had wandered freely from the tranquil slopes, in a hiss of scraping pebbles.

In a rare moment of calm the envoy's sap met his eyes as the hot hart breath ejected from his steaming nostrils like a censer smoke.

E. stood in the doorway hardly daring to move in case he bolted into *ether*. The scout stood listening to his every single syllable hypnotized by poppy. He became conscious of the warbling of the heavens. The stronger the song the greater the element. His soft waters floated over turbulence...and situated below his forehead were two amethysts.

'Before the harvlest fall of Adam I sound the Year of Ambridge for I love all that is pure and in my resurrection reign supreme.

Beyond the North Wind I carried the secret wall of age. The basin that never runs dry.

I was clothed in a sea of treacherous malice. My teeth tainted figureheads at the table. I split the atoms of my bitterment.

Nine great atrocities on the down-beddd larch. On the ninth day I died and was taken in. Out of darkness I wandered from the child.

52